DEVELOP

Art EXPERIENCE

4-13

MARGARET MORGAN
and
GILLIAN ROBINSON

 Nash Pollock
Publishing

Acknowledgements

Thanks are due to: John Fulton, for contributing the foreward to this publication; Stanley Thornes Ltd for permission to use excerpts from *Art 4–11*, by Margaret Morgan; Michael Chase for permission to reproduce 'Abruzzi Before Dusk'; Tim Wilson, Art Advisory Teacher, Suffolk for his generous support and help; Rebecca Sinker for contributing The Rosendale Odyssey; Diana Jenkins and all the staff at Rosendale Infants for their continuing enthusiasm and support; The National Gallery for permission to use 'The Castle at Muiden' by Jan Beerstraten; Julia Page, Art Adviser for Enfield, for her encouragement and support; Eleanor Debney, David Downes, Amber Guy-Robinson, Lisa Nicholas, Alice Turner and Claire Williams, for permission to use their work; Garth Tomkins for photography on pp 28, 66–7; the teachers and others who contributed work, reported or wrote material for the projects, or supported the venture in other ways: Duncan Allan, Jo Barnard, Greg Beavis, Wendy Benest, Norah Buckley, Janet Churcher, Jackie Clarke, Moira Connell, Christine Cooper, Sue Cooper, Lyn Corderoy, Jo Cross, Juliet Croyden, Lisa Debney, Maggie East, Anne Fletcher, Fiona Guy-Robinson, Judy Gypp, Ralph Hawkins, Jo Itter, Mary Lawrence, Ruth Mezits, Joan Minns, Fiona Pay, Sally Pitcher, Leonora Pruett, Graham Robinson, Jackie Rodger, Jim Sillett, Caroline Turner, Tanya Twigg, Natasha Warnes, Andrew Webber, Helen Whiter, Gwyneth Williams, Steve Wilson and Pauline Woraker. The headteachers, staff and children from the following schools: Baddow Junior School, Baddow, Essex; Belstead Special School, Ipswich, Suffolk; Birchwood County Primary School, Ipswich, Suffolk; Brecknock Primary School, Camden, London; Broomsgrove County Junior School, Clacton-on-Sea, Essex; Colneis Junior School, Felixstowe, Suffolk; Farlingaye High School Woodbridge, Suffolk; Highwoods County Primary School, Colchester, Essex; Holland Park Primary School, Holland-on-Sea, Essex; The Latymer School, London Borough of Edmonton; The Mary Bassett Lower School, Leighton Buzzard, Bedfordshire; Ranelagh County Primary School, Ipswich, Suffolk; Riddlesworth Hall School, Diss, Norfolk; St John's Green School, Colchester, Essex; St Pancras RCVA Primary School, Ipswich, Suffolk; Stowmarket Middle School, Suffolk; Tattingstone CEVP Primary School, Ipswich, Suffolk; Thomas Mills High School, Framlingham, Suffolk; Thundersley County Infants School, South Benfleet, Essex; Torpoint Community School, Torpoint, Cornwall; Writtle Junior School, Essex.

© 1997 Margaret Morgan and Gillian Robinson
First published in 1997 by
Nash Pollock Publishing
32 Warwick Street
Oxford OX4 1SX

10 9 8 7 6 5 4 3 2 1

Orders to
9 Carlton Close
Grove
Wantage
Oxfordshire OX12 0PU

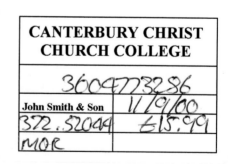

A catalogue record for this book is available from the British Library

ISBN 1 898255 16 4

Design, typesetting and production by Black Dog Design, Buckingham.
Colour origination by Advance Laser Graphic Arts, Hong Kong.
Printed in Hong Kong by Wing King Tong Co. Ltd.

Contents

Dedication

Dedicated to Seonaid Robertson whose words of wisdom and value in art education have withstood the test of time;

to Tim Wilson whose apt description of the need for 'lighting-up time' prior to children making art has caught the imagination of so many teachers;

and to all teachers and children who continue to work in the living tradition of art education.

Foreword

This very welcome book acknowledges the pleasure which we as parents and teachers share in the inventiveness of children's ideas and imagery. The authors urge us to add to this delight a deeper understanding, of how the vitality of children's imagery may be both sustained and developed through enlightened teaching. They warn us against a too-ready attachment to personal preferences in our judgements of art, and offer us a most helpful and rational structure for teaching pupils who come to us with a range of differing perceptions and abilities.

Teachers who wish merely to dip into this book, to seek what is appropriate for pupils at a particular stage, will certainly find such guidance, but they may well be beguiled to read on by the promise of seeing their lessons as part of a continuous process for developing pupils' experience of art. Those who fully adopt the authors' suggestions can expect responsive outcomes which will satisfy the requirements and aspirations of the National Curriculum.

The book will provoke some readers to raise for themselves interesting questions about whether art itself makes progress and where the realism of one culture becomes the symbolism of another. However there is no doubt that art teaching modelled, as it is here, upon the language and well-honed study methods of artists and designers enables pupils to heighten their perceptions of the real world, to advance their critical awareness and to raise their practical standards. It is this conviction, based upon their extensive knowledge of what works with children, which enables the authors to inspire and guide teachers through this book, to achieve a successful programme for their own pupils.

The nature of authentic practice is explained and detailed within the text and is also effectively summarised upon three broadsheet matrices which relate to each of the three key stages covered here. Curricular objectives and suggested roles for teachers are linked to language and to the formal elements of art and design. These presentations are most impressive feature of the book and I am confident that they will become a highly valued and lasting resource for very many teachers.

John Fulton
Art and Design Consultant

Tonal tree. 13 years

INTRODUCTION

White flowers. 11 years

This book is built around the premise that art education is a vital component in the life of every human being.

We must of course put this statement to the test, and in support of our case we would argue that any education which is to stand our children in good stead for whatever needs and developments the future may present should enable them to understand and use the potential of all aspects of human response and experience. The mental, physical and spiritual; the rational and intuitive; the subjective and objective; the cognitive and affective – or whatever headings we decide to use in dividing up the whole gamut of human response – should encourage us to respect a deeper understanding of all ways of working. We need each of these aspects in order to function fully. Art experience in fact comes across uniquely, as well as stimulating and enriching other disciplines and aspects of learning. Many of the world's greatest figures would not have been able to play their significant parts if they had not used their capacities and gifts to the fullest extent. A few examples spring to mind such as Archimedes, Hildegard of Bingen, Mahatma Ghandi, Leonardo da Vinci, Albert Einstein, Henri Poincaré, William Blake, Paul Nash, Thomas Edison, Yehudi Menuhin, Martha Graham, JMW Turner, Ludwig Van Beethoven. Creativity knows no restrictions in functioning, and can move from insight to imagining, from rational to intuitive thinking, to practice, to consideration, in whichever order or repeating sequence is appropriate.

If we were to consider the ascendency of the rational only, as some curricular documentation might suggest, we would be offering a limited tool indeed for the future needs of the world and the individuals who live in it.

When we used the word 'vital' in our initial statement in relation to art education and the needs of the human being, we did so with due consideration. The dictionary (Chambers) describes it in the context in which we wish to use it as 'supportive' or 'necessary to life', 'essential', 'energetic', 'capable of living', 'living', 'the manifestation of organic life'. We believe that art education can fit all of these definitions.

If art, which is preverbal and non-verbal (unless we choose to talk about it), can be seen as a particular vehicle for the development of the whole person, and we take into account the intrinsic activities of experiencing, thinking, feeling and acting, the possibilities for development are endless. Many teachers will cite examples of children's whole way of working and qualitative practice being changed following successful involvement.

Every child from the so-called 'mainstream' or those with 'special educational needs' (including gifted children) is a member of our society, and as such has a right to our respect and care. There can be no place for undifferentiated groups of 'failures' who have not been enabled to understand ways forward from the point they have reached. If our so-called low achievers are seen as a yardstick to prove the qualities of the 'achievers', then as teachers we will have failed. We believe that children of all abilities should leave each teacher, phase or school with a realistic and hopeful vision of positive and possible ways forward, and avenues they might follow and explore for future interests and developments. Children need to be introduced to their own vision of future possibilities – in Robin Tanner's words 'be introduced to themselves'. Surely the real mark of a good teacher is what a child, however young, is able to do on leaving the supportive presence.

One of the great strengths of teachers of young children has been their ability and skill to see each child's education as a balanced whole, to diagnose stages reached, and to put into place appropriate support and challenge. They are aware that children learn holistically rather than in fragmented and isolated disciplines taught separately. The latter approach has led to the need to contrive integration. We believe that particular disciplines are important, but unless they are seen in the context of the whole their true value can be undermined. Teachers also need to be able to weld the curriculum in such a manner that continuity, development and wholeness can be clearly experienced. Fragmentation does not lead to sound developmental education either in particular disciplines, or across the curriculum.

In art and design in particular, fragmentation weakens educational value, and it is to attempt to point to more positive ways of working that this book has been compiled. The creation of end products without due respect for process, and the imposition of isolated skills out of context, can lead to the collection of a number of items in a folder; but may show no evidence of exploration, experimentation and usage in appropriate contexts, or the steady development which leads children to make their own decisions and act on them. It is useful to remember that one of the final objectives outlined in Key Stage 3 is for children to 'work independently' and this needs nurture and expert teaching at each of the earlier stages to enable them to do it. From the earliest years it is crucial to encourage children to play with materials. In fact *research* is a word which might well be used for this exploratory and experimental work as they are building up the language and understanding for using resources in later work. It is also important to nurture each child's natural desire to key in their own experiences of the world about them, their homes, families, friends, interests and feelings. If we can harness these very personal approaches, feeding and broadening experience by sound teaching, some very rewarding things can happen. By sound teaching we mean providing a good working environment, appropriate materials, much rich first-hand experience and stimuli; the ability to gain children's interest, and to interact with them, in order to enable each one to develop to the fullest extent.

Owl. 12 years

Armadillo. 13 years

It is important of course to see that our challenges are appropriate to the experience and ability of the children, but we must also take care not to underestimate them and box them into our own self-fulfilling prophesies. Open-ended challenges allow room for growth, and often the same challenge to children of differing age or ability groups is naturally responded to at each child's own level. This is the soundest kind of differentiation. Skilfull support as children proceed with the work can enable further development. The National Curriculum exhortation to offer children simple challenges needs careful thought and we should beware of possible pitfalls. We cannot help being reminded of an excerpt from a primary teacher's notebook found in a junk shop and dated 1910. Clearly she had to deal with menus too, and liver, potatoes and cabbage feature weekly, together with the current prices! One wondered whether it was the highlight of the week or a relaxed last gasp, but Friday afternoons were art afternoons. The plans were succinct, and she clearly had to find suitable material for the whole school. Thus two consecutive weeks read as follows:

March 7th 'Older children – draw a hen from memory. Infants – draw an egg'
March 14th 'Older children – draw a wheelbarrow. Infants – draw a wheel'

Hopefully our children will feel confident to attempt anything, and have the vigour and interest to do so. When confidence and the knowledge that what they do is taken seriously and respected, whether or not it worked at first attempt, leaps of imagination and learning, or the first sequence of developmental steps, can take place.

To balance our well-meaning teacher of 1910, there is a lovely example of a five year old girl who had no such hang ups of what she should or should not be able to do. She loved stories of all kinds and presented the teacher with a tiny drawing in pencil and pink crayon. It consisted of a humanoid shape – a somewhat triangular head (or was it perhaps a head/body), string like legs, a pointed hat, and criss-cross lines for each of the eyes (the only feature depicted). 'That', she said pointing to the figure, 'is the magician with the reflection of the princess in his eyes.' Her self-imposed stimulus was a gripping story. We should not underestimate the power of language to engage children in creative work: whether it is descriptive, expressive, poetry or prose it can be a trigger for memory, imagination or illuminating source materials and first-hand experience.

As well as a rich diet of words a major component of present day teaching lies in the experience of looking at artefacts and design forms (ideally at first hand) and in meeting artists, craftspeople and designers. In the first place the most important thing this can do is to introduce teachers and children working together to the fact that there are many different valid ways of making art and of designing. It also shows that it is a serious business for adults to communicate and express what they see, or have feelings – either good or disturbing – about. Other aspects show them responding to materials, shapes, line, texture, form, light and shade, or designing and making for specific needs. Children do not find it hard to be interested in or to identify with works of art, craft, or design, and it is as valid for them to dislike as to like them. The real questions of Why? What? When? Where? How? If? can prove useful challenges for further thought and information to emerge, and it is useful for them to talk about their own work and practices as well. The common factors between adult and children's work at its best is the personal statement, the driving interest, the 'message', the interest in decoration, or in the case of functional design the response to a particular need. If we can introduce children in a positive way to this new world, and the potential and enjoyment of their own work, we are well on the way to offering them an effective education.

We hope the examples of practice in this book illustrate the strength of work seen as a continuum where one challenge naturally leads to another, and a steady developmental programme can be seen running through the teaching, thinking, response and further motivation. Clearly teachers have had to watch the overview and balance of the work to see that all necessary aspects are covered within the curriculum, and this balancing may well have taken place outside the practice presented here.

The National Curriculum need not be limiting, in fact it has much to offer, but it should be seen for what it is – a sound skeletal plan. Skeletons of all kinds need flesh and blood to enable them to live, and above all they need a heart. There is a place for the enthusiasms of teachers and children, and it is only when the whole thing is a living vital energy that interest, joy, light and (in the best sense of the word) love can be generated. It is at this point that one thing can lead to another and to the self-reward of children and teachers.

We should have confidence in what we know is there within our children, and our aim should always be to keep them in touch with the reality and validity of personal experience, and their own potential to deal with any challenge which might arise.

Tortoise. 11 years

Part I

1 The developing curriculum

IMAGERY AND DEVELOPMENT

We believe that an understanding of the way in which childrens' imagery develops, taking into account the significance of particular characteristics and ways of working, lies at the heart of enlightened teaching in the early years.

A sound pattern of development will show that children work in three ways:

Exploration and experimentation, which includes manipulation of tools and materials, and scribble;

Symbolism, where children depict what they know, what involves them on a particular moment of a particular day, and where the hierarchy of scale often accords to interest rather than to visual reality;

Visual Realism, an analytical approach where children look, touch, record and interpret, based on first-hand experience.

These modes of working are very much in line with the findings of art educationists and teachers past and present, but the inference that children pass through the first two stages and remain constant in the third is questionable.

We believe that the majority do build up experience in this order, but that far from passing through a stage, to be able to make the most of their creative working they can quite naturally retain all three modes, and continue to use them fruitfully and interactively for as long in life as they practise art, craft and design.

Exploration and experimentation

These can play a part in continually broadening and deepening experience of the potential of materials, tools, and ideas to express and communicate, and they can be of immense value to the practising artist, let alone our school age participants. They are an ongoing means of development and learning.

Symbolism

This is a valid form of picture and pattern making. It is also a kind of shorthand which can convey powerful messages and analogies, building up schema in the context of story telling, religious meaning of all kinds, and in communication and expression in a wide variety of forms. Many adult artists and designers use this mode of working. Examples might include Kandinsky, Miro, Klee, Chagall, Sonia Delaunay, and the Surrealist artists, Egyptian paintings, Maori and Aboriginal art, the makers and builders of art and architecture of the Christian, Buddhist, Hindu and Moslem traditions. We see it too in heraldry, signmaking and logo designs. It is interesting to note that much designing depends on selecting relevant characteristics and depicting them in the context in which they can be developed, modified, and used.

Visual realism and analysis

Sunflower. 12 years

Children and artefacts

Buds. 13 years

Happily it is now an accepted necessity in art education for the introduction of all kinds of art, craft, and design forms from the very beginning of the school experience, supported by the possibilities of meeting or working with artists, designers and craftspeople. The main purpose is to communicate to the children that there are many different ways of making art, craft and design forms, designs and designing. The experiences will have done their work if they help to overcome the insidious (though often unspoken) message that can be built up within the school, or at home, namely that photographic realism is what we are all really aiming for in the end, and that it alone is our yardstick and our norm. How many young children have been turned off art by adults, or their peers who have been blind in regard to qualities of the symbolist, and to the 'language' of colour, line, shape, texture, pattern, tone, form and space, composition, expressive strength and powerful communication. More difficult still to help to see real value are the children who bring inappropriate judgement to their own work.

Visual realism and analysis is the basis of much art world wide, past and present. For the young child the roots lie within the experience leading to symbolism, and develops with ever-deepening perception until it moves into a realm of its own where it is harnessed to become a tool for research, or a vehicle for communication or expression. The particular 'message' expressed goes way beyond the 'photographic' image if it is to become an art form because human involvement, energy and thought can give it a particular impact of its own. Examples of work based on this mode are endless and include the Benin Bronzes, Durer, Leonardo, Rembrandt, Velasquez, Constable, the Pre-Raphaelites, Manet, the Impressionists, The Post Impressionists, Van Gogh, the Expressionists, the Realists, Lucian Freud, Elizabeth Blackadder, Jacob Epstein and Elizabeth Frink.

It is very important that children should at as early a stage as possible be encouraged to enter into dialogue with the teacher and with one another in responding to artefacts and designed forms. They should feel free to talk of their likes and dislikes, and to be led to a secure understanding that there are many different ways of doing things. As teachers we should be quite clear that we are not teaching taste from a hidden agenda, but are broadening experience, and helping children to see that there are many differing criteria which can be brought to bear as well as likes and dislikes.

The ways in which teachers respond to children talking about their own and others work is of course crucial, and in the first place listening skills are most important. The whole experience is one in which language and communication skills come to the fore. The more a teacher can tune in to the child's expectation and self-constructed (or influenced) value systems, the greater the possibility for appropriate challenge and development becomes.

Perhaps the initial response from children on being introduced to works of art, craft and design, is of immediate likes, or dislikes, and the teacher will need to introduce the question 'Why do you say that?' and leading into other interrogatives – What? How? When? If? It is important too to encourage children to look again, think again, and to describe the work and their feelings. It is very interesting to see how quickly concentration spans of looking before speaking can build up under sensitive teaching.

If we are afraid that young children will not understand adult descriptions of art it is interesting to show children collections and groups of kinds of work and to challenge them to find appropriate descriptive terms. The results of one teacher working with her class are as follows. She had made collections of ten pieces of work which she felt were typical of :

a Exploration and experimentation (these included abstracts)

11

b Symbolist work

c Visual realism and analytical works

Each group of work was introduced to the children and they were given time to respond and discuss them. They were then challenged to find a good descriptive term for each group. In this instance the results were as follows:

Adult description	*Children's description*
a Exploration and experimentation (including abstracts)	'pattern pictures'
b Pictures and models which have recognisable content in symbolist mode	'story pictures'
c Visually real and analytically based work	'story pictures' 'matching pictures'

Having made quite sure that language and understanding are at one, and that children really are aware of different ways of working, we must be careful in the way in which we communicate specific challenges to them. For the very young child, as well as at times for older children, their own enthusiasm and energy carries them into rich self-motivated work, but it seldom if ever happens in a vacuum. It is the ethos and value of the overall classroom practice, the teacher's input into an interesting classroom environment, and provision of good tools and materials which is the driving force. However, when we wish to introduce particular challenges we need to consider what we are asking them to do, the reason which lies behind it, and how we intend to offer appropriate stimulation.

CONTENT AND DEVELOPMENT

The elements of art

The elements are to art what words are to verbal communication and expression. If this is understood to be true, the subject matter and the child's natural maturation in regard to imagery is not exclusively important in assessing what is really happening in art and design education. The elements of line, colour, pattern, texture, tone, form and space are the very means by which the subject matter and the imagery are communicated and expressed. It is small wonder that they are sometimes termed 'the language of art'.

If this is so, clearly we should build up the ability to understand this language and its potential and to encourage and enable young children to use it effectively. The moment, however that it takes over as a self-conscious foolproof technique we can know that it has gone too far and become an end in itself rather than a means to an end. The valid end can be seen to be personal exploration and experimentation, communication, expression and general usage.

A reasonable way to educate children in the elements of art is to focus on a particular area of experience and lead them through a

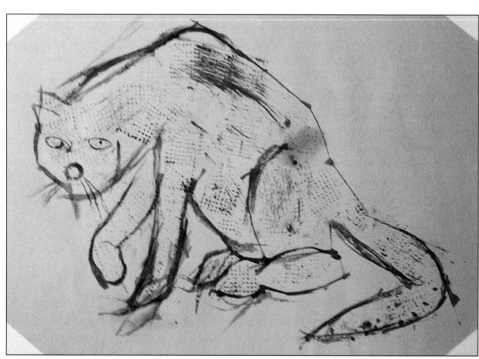

Printed cat. 11 years

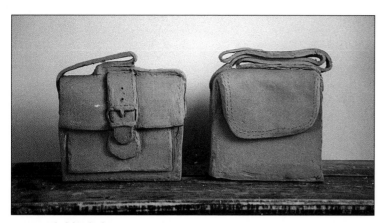

Bags. Slabbed clay. 12 years

programme of exploration, experimentation and usage. (This idea is developed in the matrix on pp 16–17.) In using this approach it is of course necessary for the children to be aware of what they are doing, and the nature and potential of the focus. Discussion is invaluable. It will soon become apparent too, that when focusing on one element others are also included quite naturally. For example, in a project on colour, when a collection of fabrics were selected for their colour qualities, pattern, shape and texture were quite naturally involved. Sound teaching will take into account overlaps of two or more elements in one piece of work. Probably the least useful way of handling it would be to feel that each element had to be painstakingly worked through in isolation and the sum total only put together when this had been achieved. It is useful to remember that one of the strengths of the child's way of working is its ability to experience holistically, and anything we might do to destroy this to the extent that we then have to introduce them to reintegrating the parts is questionable. Individual parts can be introduced and focused upon, but we should never lose sight of the whole which is already there. As children develop understanding of the vocabulary of the elements they can readily discuss them in the context of their own work and that of others.

The secret is to see that our challenges prior to exploration and experimentation are lively and enthusiastic, and that we have supplied appropriate materials and tools for rewarding involvement. Clearly there is something amiss if children's response to colour and pigment can only be experienced through the use of poor quality paint and inferior brushes! The materials should be really vibrant and satisfying to handle.

Vehicle and content

In order to enable us to have the flexibility to keep our curriculum lively and yet to structure it in a developmental form, it is important to understand the difference in terms between vehicle and content.

Put at its most basic, content refers to the art content – the language of art, the elements of line, colour, tone, pattern, texture, form and space.

The vehicle is the project or subject by which you travel this particular content road. For example, if the content is 'colour' it could be based initially on 'media exploration' and 'experimentation'. Following this a vehicle from the many possibilities might be selected: for instance this could be an environmental study based on the season of autumn which might move into paintings in response to first-hand experience, listening to poems, printmaking on fabrics, collages etc. Whatever is chosen, the vehicle is the agent by which the content is delivered.

Some vehicles need to be planned for in good time in order to amass resources and stimuli of all kinds, books and visual material, but there are other times when the enthusiasm of the moment can be slotted in to the appropriate content challenge. The skills of teaching will of course play a crucial role which we shall consider in Chapter 3.

THE NATIONAL CURRICULUM

The National Curriculum is a very human document if we bring it to life. It is a little like the 17th century cookery books which contained many recipes for breadmaking which proved to be a disaster when put to the test by present day cooks. It was only when it was realised that all early cooks knew that breadmaking required yeast, and that it was therefore not necessary to write it in, that enlightenment dawned and some excellent loaves resulted.

The 'yeast' in the National Curriculum context is the life and energy of the children, the teacher, and the dynamic and interest of the curriculum content and the vehicles for presenting it.

First and foremost we should consider its developmental nature. On pp 16-17 we have laid out the three Key Stages in columns so that it is easy to see the build up of experience and challenge.

Second, we are again and again required to work from direct experience, observation and imagination. The importance of offering children experience from reality – the visit, real items and experiences of all kinds being taken into the school and the classroom – cannot be underestimated. There can be no substitute. Sensory learning, observation, perceiving by visual and tactile means, feeling response, imagination and memory stimuli are all on-going components.

This curriculum is based on the reality of each child's experience, one stage leading to the next. It is very interesting to note that at Key Stage 3, together with the build up of skills and experience, there is an unequivocal statement that the child should 'work independently'. As we all know informed independence does not just happen at any given point, but needs to be a goal to work towards, we believe, from the beginning of Key Stage 1. For children to be able to be independent they would need to be encouraged to think and act for themselves throughout.

Following the National Curriculum outline we have worked on an example of what we consider to be appropriate *content* guidance together with the kind of information we believe would be useful for teachers to consider (pp 18-23). We are not suggesting that this is the only way of planning and presenting of the curriculum, or that this any kind of definitive 'answer'. We hope that it may be of use in furthering teachers' own thinking and discussion.

The next development required from this, or any other content scheme, is a strategy for putting into place the *vehicles* – the subject matter, particularly experiences, resources and stimuli by which the content is delivered.

It is necessary to plan ahead, especially where visits need arranging and resources need ordering or collecting. It is also necessary to look at specific areas of work where challenges might be repeated (in different guises) to look at continuity and development. We would nevertheless hope that much of what was used would ride on the immediacy of interests generated at particular times, and if a helicopter were to land in the school grounds then the moment should be fully lived, whether it be through perception and drawing, sketchbook work and note taking, or excitement expressed immediately afterwards in vivid memory paintings, or model making and designing. 'Seize the opportunity' is no bad motto for the art and design curriculum.

We also believe that within the spectrum of challenges and developments which we build up on the structure of our curriculum planning there is a place for experiences which can be looked at quite specifically by teachers, and which can help in analysing what is happening to the individual child. We need to have evidence as to whether there is in fact any development, and to see where weaknesses and strengths lie. It should be pointed out that alongside these pieces of work the sketchbook, if it is being really well handled, is an invaluable tool, not only for children's learning, but also for the teacher in assessing. In it we can look for the development of imagery – living things, people, animals, plants, trees, buildings of all sorts, machinery, imaginative and fantastic ideas, and materials exploration and experimentation. Hopefully we shall see a steady build up of confidence and skills. If we do not see this happening, we should review our own teaching strategies. In assessing any childrens' work it is important to look at both the imagery and the handling of the elements of art. They are of course interdependent, but it is by means of those elements that the message is conveyed as an art form, otherwise we may find ourselves assessing childrens' natural maturation in regard to images, and not taking the art education into account at all.

We are reminded of the work of a whole school where each child had been given the challenge of drawing themselves or a person known to them. Tools and materials had been provided, but teachers had not been given any guidance as to what or how much to say when introducing the subject to the children. The purpose was to look at the development of art practice. From the results, all of which were displayed one afternoon after school as a massive 'pavement gallery' on the floor in the hall, an interesting sequence was apparent. The criteria which the staff finally came up with was to assess the children's ability to draw figures with appropriate parts, details and awareness of proportion. No attention was given to the handling of the tools and elements.

Predictably enough, by the teachers' criteria the children 'improved' with age, but they may well have done so by maturation anyway, and it needs to be remembered that our young symbolists have their own reasons for not including all the parts they know people have if they are communicating particular messages on a particular day! When it was suggested that the elements of art were considered – the qualities of line, colour, tone and pattern for example, the staff realised that awareness of the art content was almost non-existent. In fact the reception class showed greater vigour and handled colour with greater confidence than any later work, which seemed to become more tentative and insecure as the children moved up the school.

The other factor which was self-evident was the teacher input. Clearly some teachers had said an absolute minimum and it would appear with little enthusiasm, and it seemed that the children had complied with the request without enthusiasm. In other cases what appeared to be the same challenge delivered with enthusiasm resulted in livelier work.

Those teachers who had added further challenge through taught content ranged from at best perceptive and personal work, to the other end of the scale, a prescriptive teacher-dominated approach which was apparent in slavish proportion, rules and fractions, with rather dead drawings, and one particular set where drawing gimmicks and ways of depicting features and parts of the body had clearly been demonstrated on the board. All the children's work conformed to identical symbols!

Ways forward for this school included a much greater involvement in materials exploration and experimentation, a deeper involvement in perceptive work from first-hand experience, and development of working in response to artefacts, especially in looking at the ways in which drawings and paintings were carried out.

The notion of a whole school undertaking particular challenges can be very useful. It can, providing teachers really are willing to look at the work and the teaching inferences critically, be a very powerful ground from which to move forward. It is excellent in terms of inservice experience, and can help new teachers to see particular aspects of the work in sequence.

This idea can lead on to the idea of a whole school or class building a periodic focus into the curriculum – an aspect, for example, of visual perception, where work can be looked at not only in a whole-school context, but also in the context of pieces of work which the children have undertaken at previous points in their art education. This should of course, never be introduced as a 'test', and if used should quite naturally take its place in the normal sequence of art practice.

Some excerpts from The National Curriculum, aligned in columns, making clear the developmental nature of the structure.

ART

KEY STAGE 1

Investigating & making

Pupils should be given opportunities to	Pupils should be taught to
A Record responses including observations of the natural and made environment.	**a** Record what has been experienced, observed and imagined.
B Gather resources and materials using them to stimulate and develop ideas.	**b** Recognise images and artefacts as sources of ideas for their work. **c** Select and sort images and artefacts and use this source material as a basis for their work.
C Explore and use two and three dimensional media working on a variety of scales.	**d** Experiment with tools and techniques for drawing, painting, printmaking, collage and sculpture, exploring a range of materials including textiles. **e** Experiment with visual elements (pattern, texture, colour, line, tone, shape, form and space) to make images and art forms using the range of media in **d** (above).
D Review and modify their work as it progresses.	**f** Review what they have done and describe what they might change and develop in future work.

Knowledge & understanding

E Develop understanding of the work of artists, craftspeople and designers, applying knowledge to their own work.	**a** Identify in the school and the locality the work of artists, craftspeople and designers. **b** Recognise visual elements (pattern, texture, colour, line, tone, shape, form and space) in images and artefacts. **c** Recognise differences and similarities in art, craft and design from different times and places.
F Respond to and evaluate art, craft and design including their own work.	**d** Respond to the ideas, methods and approaches used in different styles and traditions. **e** Describe works of art, craft and design in simple terms and explain what they think and feel about these.

KEY STAGE 2	KEY STAGE 3
## Investigating & making	## Investigating & making
Pupils should be taught to	Pupils should be taught to
a Develop skills for recording from direct experience and imagination and select and record from first hand observation.	**a** Develop ideas from direct experience and imagination and select, record and analyse from first hand observation.
b Record observations and ideas, and collect visual evidence and information using a sketchbook.	**b** Select and record observations and ideas, and research and organise a range of visual evidence and information using a sketchbook.
c Experiment with ideas for their work suggested by visual and other source material.	**c** Experiment with and select from visual and other source material to stimulate and develop ideas for independent work.
d Experiment with, and develop control of tools and techniques for drawing, painting, printmaking, collage & sculpture, exploring a range of materials including textiles.	**d** Select from and experiment with materials, images and ideas, and extend their knowledge and experience of a range of materials, tools and techniques.
e Experiment with, and use visual elements (pattern, texture, colour, line, tone, shape, form, and space) and make images and artefacts for different purposes (using the range of media above **d**).	**e** Select from and interpret visual elements and realise their intentions in a range of media.
f Reflect on and adapt their work in the light of what they intended, and consider what they might develop in future work.	**f** Modify and refine their work and plan and make further developments in the light of their own and others' evaluation.
## Knowledge & understanding	## Knowledge & understanding
a Identify in the school and locality the materials and methods used by artists, craftspeople and designers.	**a** Recognise the diverse methods and approaches used by artists, craftspeople and designers.
b Identify how visual elements (pattern, texture, colour, line, tone, shape, form and space) are used in images and artefacts for different purposes.	**b** Identify how visual elements are used to convey ideas, feelings and meanings in images and artefacts.
c Recognise ways in which works of art, craft and design reflect the time and place in which they are made.	**c** Relate art, craft and design to its social, historical and cultural context, eg. identify codes and conventions used in different times and cultures.
d Compare the ideas, methods and approaches used in different styles and traditions.	**d** Identify how and why styles and traditions change over time and from place to place recognising the contribution of artists, craftspeople and designers.
e Express ideas and opinions, developing an art, craft and design vocabulary, and the ability to use knowledge to support views.	**e** Express ideas and opinions and justify preferences, using knowledge and an art, craft and design vocabulary.

	General pattern of development	Objectives	Input	Vocabulary	
Age **4 years** **5 years** **6 years** **7 years**	Mark making of all kinds: Rich use of media, tools and materials: Experience is largely based on kinaesthetic response: Abstract scribble and 'pattern'. Some representational symbols emerge: Naming of accidental shapes: Natural play with the elements of art: Non representational colour. Build up of symbols alongside scribble/research experience: Experimentation with tools and materials: Figures, self, houses, animals, flowers, machinery, ideas etc: Repetition of shapes and schema: Personal scale relationships: X-ray drawings: Shapes seldom overlapped: Role play: Making collections. Personal means and methods of communication and expression: Ideas, happenings, imaginings, stories, likes and dislikes: Selected detail based on experience and knowledge: Growing desire to make 'likenesses': Pleasure in materials play/experience: Representational (not necessarily matching) colour. Sometimes a drive toward visual realism causes loss of respect for symbolist work: Realism develops naturally for some, but others can move deeper into symbols & decorative work: Some handle both approaches: Designing and finding solutions through practical work: Natural collectors – items, models, drawing…	To build up confidence and enjoyment in the use of materials and tools in a lively and dynamic way. To foster willingness/ eagerness to explore a variety of materials and tools (including the hands). To build up experience through sensory learning, making and doing of all kinds. To build up confidence in approach to new situations, materials and tools. To motivate communication, and expression of personal ideas. To enable the use of the senses, especially sight and touch as a means of experience and learning. To generate working practices showing personal response and experience. To foster a lively and inventive attitude with ability to persevere through problems to conclusions. To extend understanding of the nature of art, craft and design. To foster visual and tactile discernment and discrimination. To enable experience of the strengths of working from first hand stimuli. To enable understanding of the interest and potential of working with artefacts and designed forms.	Provide a well organised and interesting working environment with natural and made items of interest displayed in an appetising way. Provide rewarding tools and materials to enable vital involvement leading to exploration and usage. Organise experiences outside the classroom. Introduce art, craft and design forms. Encourage making collections. Use language imaginatively with a strong bias toward visual and tactile description, and feeling expression. Provide good quality tools and materials and generate explorative and experimental experience. Foster respect and care for tools and materials. Challenge children to observe and record, communicate and express themselves. Introduce vital enthusiasm and interest in all kinds of art and design. Introduce items into the classroom and organise outside visits. Use visually stimulating descriptive words richly in introductions. Introduce the idea that there are many kinds of art and design. Introduce a variety of challenges which encourage different kinds of response. Encourage respect for different approaches. Build up confidence in personal decision making.	'Doing' words – making, collecting, painting, pattern, drawing, printing, modelling, scratching, sticking, pressing, squeezing etc … Naming tools and materials. Sensory words – 'looking, hearing, touching, tasting, smelling, feelings.' Response words – 'nice, nasty, happy, sad' etc. Understand terms – 'looking, seeing, exploring, mixing' etc. Names and description of colours. Descriptive words based on sensory experience and personal feelings – 'hard, soft, rough, smooth, cold, warm, bright, dull'. Understand organisational words. Understand 'explore and experiment, record, select, etc. tone, texture, form.' Visual qualities and feelings… Dark and light: Colour experience extended – linking colours and known items – 'tomato, pillar box, lemon, sunflower'. Linking textures to experience – 'like velvet, – sandpaper' etc. Line and pattern words – 'straight, curved, jagged; repeat, symmetrical, regular, irregular, overlap,' etc. Description, and response to art forms extending/ enriching vocabulary.	
National Curriculum implications Key Stage 1		Under the headings of **1** Investigating & making **2** Knowledge & understanding KEY WORDS To: Explore Use Record Review Observe Identify Imagine Respond Recognise Describe Select Experiment Sort		Recognise images and artefacts as sources of ideas for their own work. Identify art and design forms (school and locality). Recognise visual elements … Recognise differences and similarities. Respond to ideas. Describe works of art, craft and design in simple terms and explain thoughts and feelings.	

Response to artefacts and design forms	Line Pencils, chalk, pens, brushes, fingers, thread, wire etc.	Colour Pigment, paint, inks, dyes, light etc. Qualities & energies	Shape and Pattern Painted, printed, dyed, rubbed, embossed, collaged etc.	Tone Dark and light, gradation etc. pigments, light, 3D, graphic tools	Texture Collage, threads, fibres, fabrics, wood, surface qualities etc.	Form and Space 3 dimensional experience. Using rigid and malleable materials
Introduction of art and design forms of all kinds. Talking. Likes and dislikes. Personal responses. Paintings, drawings, prints, sculpture, models, ceramics, textiles and design forms. Buildings, machinery, functional objects. Discussion. Enjoyment.	Exploration and enjoyment of graphic tools – fingers, pencils, chalk, crayon, brushes, etc. Mark making scribble and naturally developed symbols/figures. Exploration and experimentation using a wide range of tools, materials and surfaces. Embodying seen and experienced ideas, & building up ways of representing their own world and understanding.	Rewarding exploration and enjoyment. Rich thick pigment (generally mixed by the teacher, and varying in colour from time to time). Collecting coloured items – sorting, selecting, collaging. Personal expression.	Exploration. Non figurative work, collections – choosing, grouping, painting, drawing, collage, print. Awareness of surface pattern. Abstract and repeating work. Arrangements of natural and made items. Shape awareness and recognition.	Awareness of darks and lights. Collections and assemblages. Arrangements.	Exploration. Handling, manipulating and enjoying sensory experience and using materials. Awareness of surfaces and textures. Collections, sorting, pattern making, collages, reliefs.	Exploration, handling and feeling. Sensory experience. Collections – choosing. Manipulating materials. Using hands as tools. Embodiment of personal ideas. Modelling, assembling, constructing. Malleable and rigid materials. Sticking and joining.
Response to art and design forms in the school and locality. Likes and dislikes with reasons. Beginning identification. Relating ideas to their own work. Art and design forms of all kinds. Visits to artists and designers, or inviting them to school. Personal responses. Awareness of the elements of art in the works, and of different times and places.	Growing awareness of natural and made environment: Challenges to look and SEE, remember and imagine: First hand experience recorded and ideas expressed. Looking at shapes, pattern, tone, texture, line, form. Expressive and imaginative work: Understanding, respecting and enjoying realist, symbolist, pattern and abstract work. Engaging personal interest and feelings. Looking at drawings. Working out ideas. Sketchbooks.	Awareness of the variety of colours in the environment and in art, craft and design forms of all kinds. Rich exploration of colours, and experimentation. Using colour. Personally experienced subject matter. Work from memory, imagination and direct visual experience. Mixing and discussing effects. Colour displays. Mixing and matching. Responding to colour experience from artefacts etc.	Exploration and experimentation with tools and techniques. Arranging repeating, folding, overlapping. Regular and irregular patterns. Patterns in nature, and the made world of art and design – textiles, furnishing, buildings, decorative objects. Print, paint, dyes, textile construction. Using a wide range of materials.	Exploration of darks and lights. Displays. Collections of ranges of tone – whites/grays/black. Ranges based on one colour. Sorting, selecting, arranging and rearranging. Collage, paint, drawing tools etc.	Awareness of surface qualities. Searching, recording, selecting, rubbing and relief. Exploration and experimentation. Developing panels, reliefs, hangings and constructions etc.	Awareness of natural and made forms and environments. Direct modelling and hand built forms. Displays. Materials-generated ideas. Work from direct visual and touch stimuli, personal feelings and experiences. Building/making models, reliefs, constructions. Using hands and tools. Use of adhesives.
Identify local artists and works … Recognise visual elements, differences and similarities … Respond to different styles and methods … Describe works simply, … and their own feelings…	Record what has been experienced, observed, imagined. Experiment with tools and techniques for drawing … exploring a range of materials. Experience and recognise visual elements.	EXPLORE EXPERIMENT REVIEW USE	EXPLORE EXPERIMENT REVIEW USE	EXPLORE EXPERIMENT REVIEW USE	EXPLORE EXPERIMENT REVIEW USE	EXPLORE EXPERIMENT REVIEW USE

	General pattern of development	Objectives	Input	Vocabulary	
Age **8 years** **9 years** **10 years** **11 years**	Evidence of greater knowledge of their world: Direct experience: Dramatic happenings, everyday life: Interest in detail and sections as well as wholes: Greater dependence on looking: Interest in proportion: Designing and making working models: Build up of techniques: Personal interests deepening: Notebooks, sketchbooks, collections. Ability to select and use tools and materials to specific purpose. Ability to handle ideas and continue to make personal statements in abstract, symbolist, decorative and visual realist ways. Enjoying being challenged to look, explore, experiment, and use techniques. Awareness of visual depth. Without support a loss of interest and confidence can take place. Continuing to work personally and individually much of the time. Enjoying working in pairs and groups, discussing ideas and carrying out work. Evidence of understanding the potential and use of the elements of art. Awareness of mood and energies, and the form and function of work, with teacher support. Can range from sophisticated visual approach to highly personal, or idiosyncratic work. Some can lose interest unless skilfully motivated. A healthy or over-dependence and usage of other peoples imagery. Interest in art and design forms given opportunity. Ability to self motivate in and out of school. At best a good grasp of form and function.	To enable understanding of the relevence of exploration and experiment to art, craft and design practice. To build up a vocabulary of practical response with special attention to first hand experience. To foster the ability to recognise and discuss different approaches to their own and other people's work. To understand the nature of art, craft, design and designing more fully. To develop listening, discursive and communicative skills. To enable children to meet challenges positively, and to be able to select appropriate tools and materials. To enable independent thinking and action supported by the skills of researching and collecting relevant information. To build confidence, encouraging thoughtful responses and the expression of ideas, supported by reasoning and sensitive reflection.	Extend exploration, experimentation and the build up of skills. Challenge to PERCEIVE (look and touch) at an intense level. Encourage confident response and skilful communication and expression. Introduce first hand stimuli – in and out of school. Extend sketch/notebook practice. Encourage working directly with materials, stimuli, ideas, and developing personal statements – lines of research. Introduce art and design forms, artists and designers. Organise gallery visits etc. Encourage personal responses and questions WHAT, HOW? WHY? WHEN? WHERE? WHAT DO YOU THINK? Encourage links with their own work – introduce art, design, arts and cross-curricular projects with opportunities for individual, group and team work. Encourage description and appraisal of work, ability to adapt, and see inferences for the future.	Discuss the words *art, craft* and *design*. Understand words and concepts of earlier experiences. Understand 'looking and seeing,' 'analysing,' 'imagining,' 'designing,' 'mixing and matching,' sculpture, construction, modelling, collage, weaving, hangings, mobiles, mixed media, pottery, manuscript, calligraphy. Colour – hues, shades, tints. Build up listening and reading skills and ability to organise words to discuss, plan, annotate and describe ways of working and designing. Encourage the use of words to discuss, describe, analyse, compare, contrast, communicate and express feelings and thoughts naturally. Encourage making links between responses to artefacts and their own work.	
National Curriculum implications Key Stage 2		Develop skills for recording. Select and record. Record observations and ideas. Collect visual evidence. Experiment with ideas. Experiment, develop, control. Experiment and use. Reflect on, adapt. Identify how … Recognise ways in which … Compare. Express ideas and opinions.		Reflect on and adapt work… consider future developments. Identify the materials and methods of artists … Identify how visual elements are used for different purposes. Recognise how works of art differ (re time and place). Compare ideas, methods, approaches (re styles and traditions). Express opinions and support views.	

Response to artefacts and design forms	Line Pencils, chalk, pens, brushes, fingers, thread, wire etc.	Colour Pigment, paint, inks, dyes, light etc. Qualities & energies	Shape and Pattern Painted, printed, dyed, rubbed, embossed, collaged etc.	Tone Dark and light, gradation etc. pigments, light, 3D, graphic tools	Texture Collage, threads, fibres, fabrics, wood, surface qualities etc.	Form and Space 3 dimensional experience. Using rigid and malleable materials
Looking at all kinds of art and design forms. Museums and galleries. Discussing ways in which things were made, and materials and tools used. Relevance to their own work. Question why things were made/painted etc. in particular ways, and how effects have been achieved through the elements of art and design. Look for form and function, mood and message. Look at different approaches to making art and design forms at different times and places: Find reasons for working in particular ways. Look for relevence to their own ways of working. Look at different art and design forms. Express and support personal responses, ideas and opinions, using appropriate vocabulary. See relevance to their own work. Have confidence to enjoy finding out about art and design forms.	Exploration and experimentation. Developing skills for recording, expressive and decorative work from direct experience, imagination and fantasy. Experience, and recognition of elements of line, pattern, shape, texture, tone and colour. Looking at the environment and made world. Intense observation. Looking and drawing. Variation in scale. Collecting visual information. Sketchbooks. Drawing as a means of designing. Tool and material awareness – particular qualities for needs. Reflecting on practice and potential.	Exploration and experimental work with pigments, materials and light sources. Using colour to analyse, describe and express ideas, based on direct experience, imagination, communicating ideas and expressive work. Collecting visual evidence of colour. (Sketchbooks etc.) Mixing and matching. Exploration and experimentation: Controlling and using colour descriptively and expressively. Direct visual experience, memory and imagination. Qualities of colour, tone, tint, shade, hue and mood. Colour for purposes. Looking at works of art and design. Reflecting on what has been done, and on future practice.	Shape experimentation. Searching for and researching shape and pattern in the environment and made world. Sketchbook work. Paint print, collage, textiles, lettering and decoration: Positive and negative shapes. Repetition. Many layered work, over printing. Mixed media. Patterns based on the environment and made forms. Patterns for purposes (particular) – book covers, for wearing and furnishing, dolls and puppets clothes. Panels and hangings, etc. Reflecting on what has been done and on future practice.	Exploration and experimentation. Awareness of dark and light qualities and gradations in single colours. Beginning to see qualities in a range of colours. Sorting from dark to light items. Looking for potential in tools and materials. Search for tonal qualities and effects in artefacts. Tone and mood interrelationship. Paintings, drawings, patterns, collage. Reflecting on practice and talking about outcomes and potential.	Exploration and experimentation of the nature of surfaces. Relief and decoration. Searching for and recording texture and relief in natural and made contexts. Rubbing, imprinting, casting, collaging, weaving, constructing. Surface decoration. Light and shade on surfaces. Surfaces and reliefs in artefacts and designed forms. Reflect on practice and think about future developments.	Exploration, experimentation. Practical qualities and potential of malleable and constructional materials: Learning, communication, expression, problem solving. Materials-generated ideas. Working from first hand experience – Items from the environment, and artefacts/design forms. Figures, forms, groups, environments, buildings. Clay: pinching, slabbing, coiling, relief: Extending techniques in relation to needs. Understanding qualities of adhesives. Light, shadow, form and space interrelationships. Form and function. Reflecting on practice, and ways forward.
Identify materials/methods. Identify how the elements are used for purposes … Recognise the influence of time and place on art. Compare different approaches. Express ideas and opinions and support views.	Select and record – direct experience – imagination. Collect visual evidence and information (sketchbooks). Experiment with and identify visual elements. Develop control of tools and techniques … Make things … Reflect and adapt…	EXPLORE EXPERIMENT USE REFLECT and ADAPT	EXPLORE EXPERIMENT USE REFLECT and ADAPT	EXPLORE EXPERIMENT USE REFLECT and ADAPT	EXPLORE EXPERIMENT USE REFLECT and ADAPT	EXPLORE EXPERIMENT USE REFLECT and ADAPT

	General pattern of development	Objectives	Input	Vocabulary	
Age **12 years** **13 years** **14 years**	A wide range of experience, practice and confidence evident. Some children are highly visually orientated and quite naturally use art for purposes of learning, communication and expression. Others find a purely visual mode less easy to align and handle, but can often relate more readily to work generated through first hand experience of the materials and elements of art. Non figurative work and symbolism can also play a part. Three dimensional work and textural experience can be real strengths for some children. Many have the ability to work toward their own ends given sufficient stimuli. Building up collections of background material and researching can meet needs and enthusiasms. This is the optimum time for enjoyment of materials and tools, and the need to master techniques is strong. This is a stage where there is a strong need for first hand stimuli, and an important time to deepen understanding of artefacts. It is crucial that they understand the equally valid strengths of all forms of working. Some students find working in pairs and teams useful, whilst others find it very difficult.	To extend and develop experience of using a wide variety of materials through rigorous exploration, experimentation and usage. To extend and deepen understanding of relevant techniques and tools. To develop ideas from direct experience and imagination. To select and record from first hand observation using two and three dimensional material. To deepen experience of visual perception and analysis. To understand the nature and potential of the elements of art (colour, shape, pattern, line, tone, texture, form and space) and to be able to handle them effectively. To foster skills of selection. To encourage research and build up ranges of visual evidence and information [including sketchbooks]. To be able to develop work, modify and refine it, and to plan further developments. To be aware of the wide variety of art, craft and design forms, and to realise the effect time and place has on style and content. To be confident to offer personal opinions in regard to their own and others work and to be able to thoughtfully justify their conclusions.	Extend materials exploration and experimentation. Build up relevant skills and techniques. Provide a rich environment with stimulating collections of natural and made items including artefacts. Organise visits to places of interest, artists, craftspeople and designers. Deepen understanding and practice based on perception (vision and touch). Introduce media, materials and artefacts for work based on the elements of art. Introduce stimuli/resources/experiences for the build up of research. Build up evidence and information for present and future working. Extend the use of sketchbooks/folders etc. as resource tools. Teach the skills of developing ideas and work, presentation, appraisal, and the ability to refine, modify and plan for future development. Introduce the effects of time and place on artefacts and their relationships to social, historical and cultural contexts. Encourage discussion of their own and others' work. Build up confidence in their own work and opinions, and teach them to justify their conclusions. Enable independent work based on research and exploration.	Use, and build on the vocabulary introduced in earlier years. Build vocabulary around descriptions and analogies in relation to natural and made forms, around the names of artists, craftspeople and designers, schools and modes of working, and relevent technical issues. Encourage words describing visual and touch qualities, analytic descriptions, and those pertaining to feeling response. Enable the use of succinct description in planning and designing. Enable understanding of the nature of evaluation, and appropriate words to support conclusions. Enable understanding of the meaning of style and tradition in relation to art and design practice. Enlighten them on the skills of justifying their work and opinions.	
National Curriculum implications Key Stage 3		Develop ideas (self) Select, record and analyse … Research and organise … Experiment, select, develop. Work independently. Extend knowledge and experience. Select, interpret and realise. Modify, refine and plan; evaluate and develop. Identify how and why … Relate and identify … Express and justify …		Experiment with images and ideas. Plan and make. Evaluate. Recognise diverse methods and approaches. Identify how visual elements are used. Relate art to its social context. Identify how styles and traditions change. Express ideas and opinions… justify.	

Response to artefacts and design forms	Line Pencils, chalk, pens, brushes, fingers, thread, wire etc.	Colour Pigment, paint, inks, dyes, light etc. Qualities & energies	Shape and Pattern Painted, printed, dyed, rubbed, embossed, collaged etc.	Tone Dark and light, gradation etc. pigments, light, 3D, graphic tools	Texture Collage, threads, fibres, fabrics, wood, surface qualities etc.	Form and Space 3 dimensional experience. Using rigid and malleable materials
Offer wide experience of art, craft and design forms through looking at original work and reproductions. Consider methods and approaches used by artists, craftspeople and designers. Look at form, function, mood and message. Look at artforms and analyse visual elements, the ways in which effects have been achieved and ideas and feelings conveyed. Make practical studies of different methods of working. Introduce the study of art, craft and design works in relation to social, historical and cultural contexts. Consider traditions and styles and the ways in which they change in relation to time and place. Encourage expression of personal opinions and ideas, and enable them to support and justify their considerations.	Explore and experiment leading to different ways of handling the potential of linear qualities. Selecting, recording and analysing from direct experience and imagination. Build up a bank of practical material and research as a resource for future work (including sketchbook). Develop a range of techniques and see their potential. Recognise the different ways in which artists, craftspersons and designers have used linear qualities to effect. Be aware of how other elements interact with linear qualities. Encourage independent work. Reflect on what has been achieved, on ideas and ways forward.	Explore and experiment leading to interactions, subtle accuracies and purposeful mixing (pigments and light sources). Work from direct experience and imagination, selecting: expressing, recording and analysing. Build up a bank of practical work, exploration and collections for use as a research support resource (including sketchbooks). Develop and extend a whole range of relevent techniques. Recognise the potential and power of colour in art and design forms. Be aware of how the other elements interact with colour. Encourage independent work. Reflect on what has been achieved, on ideas and ways forward.	Explore and experiment leading to new ways of working, and control. Select, express, record and analyse from direct experience and imagination. Build up a bank of practical material and research as a resource for future work (including sketchbooks). Develop a range of techniques and see their potential. Be aware of the way in which other elements interact with shape and pattern. Recognise the potential of shape and pattern through studying the works of artists and designers. Encourage independent work. Reflect on what has been achieved, on ideas and ways forward.	Explore and experiment leading to different ways of handling tonal qualities. Select, record, analyse, and express ideas from direct experience and imagination. Build up a bank of practical work and research as a resource and stimuli for future projects (including sketchbooks). Develop a range of techniques. Recognise the different ways in which artists, crafts people and designers have used tone to effect. Be aware of how other elements interact with tone. Encourage independent work. Reflect on what has been achieved, on ideas and ways forward.	Explore and experiment leading to different ways of handling the potential of textural qualities. Selecting, recording and analysing from direct experience and imagination. Build up a bank of practical material and research as a resource for future work (including sketchbooks). Develop a range of techniques and see their potential. Recognise the different ways in which artists, craftspeople and designers have used texture to effect. Be aware of how other elements interact with texture. Encourage independent work. Reflect on what has been achieved, on ideas and ways forward.	Explore and experiment leading to different ways of handling the potential of form and spatial qualities. Select, record, and analyse from direct experience and imagination. Build up a bank of practical material and research as a resource for future work (including sketchbooks). Develop a range of techniques and see their potential. Recognise the different ways in which artists, craftspersons and designers have used form and space. Encourage independent work. Reflect on what has been achieved, on ideas and ways forward.
Recognise divers methods and approaches. Identify how visual elements are used to convey ideas, feelings and meanings. Relate art and design to its social, historical and cultural context. Identify why styles and traditions change … Relate experience to personal work. Express ideas and opinions and justify preferences.	EXPLORE EXPERIMENT USE REFLECT and ADAPT.	EXPLORE, EXPERIMENT, USE, REFLECT and ADAPT.	EXPLORE EXPERIMENT USE REFLECT and ADAPT.	EXPLORE EXPERIMENT USE REFLECT and ADAPT.	EXPLORE EXPERIMENT USE REFLECT and ADAPT.	EXPLORE EXPERIMENT USE REFLECT and ADAPT.

ASSESSMENT, RECORDING AND REPORTING

In this section we will look at the particular relevance of assessment in the context of a developing art experience, and ways in which it can help to shape that experience, taking into account the three indispensable basics in any consideration in regard to assessment: the child, the teacher and the work.

What are we assessing?

Assessing, recording and reporting have unavoidable judgemental overtones and are particularly sensitive areas in the context of art, especially when the art to be assessed involves personal 'feeling' responses. There is no doubt that the personal responses of each child deserve our utmost respect and are usually best assessed through sensitive dialogue. There will, however, be times when we do not share our assessment with the child, where it is enough for the child to do a piece of work and to celebrate its value rather than analysing it. This might particularly be the case with very young children. There are some aspects of learning within art which lend themselves more easily to assessment: for example children's developing ability to recognise and use in a context the elements of art – line, tone, colour, form, texture, pattern; their developing dexterity in manipulating tools; and their knowledge and appropriate use of techniques. Here it is possible, by relating closely to progression, to identify ways in which assessment can have a positive influence towards developing and facilitating a personal response.

In order to develop criteria for assessment in art it is necessary to identify and understand what it is we as art educators are about. First and foremost it is important to learn what it is that artists (both adults and children) do, and to understand that what they do is based in an inherent curiosity and in a basic need to create images and artefacts which communicate our inner feelings and our responses to the world around us. It is to do with investigating and making which is facilitated by the act of exploring, recording, observing, imagining, recognising, selecting, reviewing, identifying, responding, describing, and expressing. This is supported by the requirements of National Curriculum Attainment Target 1, and is relevant throughout the educational process.

The activities above need to be understood by seeing them as processes in relation to final art and design statements and forms. To facilitate this it is valuable to look at artists' sketchbooks, particularly where the original sketchbook is available, although where there is no alternative replica sketchbooks are also useful. This needs to be integral with an opportunity to experience and gain knowledge of a range of art and artefacts. This is supported by National Curriculum Attainment Target 2, where pupils are required to make connections between a variety of artistic traditions and their own work. Children's process work and sketchbooks serve the same purpose.

Exploration and experimentation is a sound beginning. Some exploration is in its own right and deals with learning about the 'language' of art: line, tone, form, colour, texture, and pattern. Some experimentation leads into a range of art or artefacts which has been triggered by the experiment. In the kinds of challenge introduced, one should begin to see the fruits of the exploration/experimentation which is building up all the way along. Sometimes the child initiates the challenge. An example of this may be following first-hand experience which is unique to that child: a birthday party or a trip to a wildlife park. At other

School bus. Special school. 9 x 15 cms

Jay. 9 years. 10 x 20 cms

times the teacher will initiate the challenge for a specific purpose – for example colour experience. These 'specific purposes' are some of the ingredients of assessment criteria for they will have as part of their planning and structure a set of learning objectives against which the process and the end product can be assessed.

In the light of assessment, the teacher can see how the child has used the involvement with materials and his or her developing perception in ongoing work. In order to further develop the child's experience we aim to enable them to use this accumulation of learning in many different contexts, enriching the symbolist with interests and inner vision and enriching those who most naturally work from memory and the visually real by stories and by surrounding them with interesting things to look at and touch, for it is vital that the language of art for each child is a means of expression and communication of ideas and feelings which are sensitive and dynamic.

Through meaningful dialogue which recognises and respects the child's opinions, we can show our genuine interest in what the child seeks to communicate. In this way the more difficult part of assessment in art, the creative and personal aspect, can be addressed.

The child as assessor

One of the aims of art education, and consequently of the assessment process in art, is to encourage a level of autonomy for each child so that they are able to value art as an activity and themselves as individuals.

Children should be offered strategies for making informed judgements about their own work and with which to respond appropriately to the work of others. This should be an ongoing process where, within a framework of exploration and experimentation with both materials and ideas and their ultimate use, the notion of constantly reviewing one's work, by reflecting upon it and adapting accordingly, should be seen as part of the artist's methodology. Children should be encouraged to feel part of this tradition and identify with the role of artist. It is then appropriate for them to use reflection and assessment as a formative tool to develop personal response through informed choice of materials and approach.

This implies also that the child has a vocabulary of relevant art terms with which to discuss alternatives; and has put into practice, seen and talked about a range of art and artefacts including that of their peers. We have considered matters of vocabulary in the Key Stage matrices (pp 18-23).

The role of the teacher as assessor

For the teacher, teaching and assessment is a continuum. Neither the initial stimuli or the assessment can be achieved without the teacher ingredient of enthusiasm and insight into the nature of children and the nature and elements of art itself.

The role of the teacher can be seen to be that of creating a working environment where making and learning about art is irresistible.

An awareness of the following things can help towards the creation of the teacher ethos which is a necessary context for any learning but particularly necessary in providing a context for art:

- a clear/sound knowledge of the individual needs of children in the class
- a challenging task at the right level for individual children
- children who are motivated and stimulated
- good planning which provides continuity

- clear instructions which can be understood
- children who know the stages of the task
- children who have reasonable autonomy and who know how to care for materials
- clear boundaries and fair expectations
- a relaxed and calm atmosphere
- communication with, and support from, parents.

Teachers as assessors are required to put themselves into the place of the assessed. From this position they should ask relevant questions such as: Was the stimulus or starting point relevant? Were appropriate materials and sufficient space made available? Was there enough time allowed for the task?

Children should also be helped to ask these questions for themselves and encouraged to discuss their findings.

With these things in place, criteria for assessment can be addressed. Clearly there could be differing requirements for different age groups and organisation but the following areas need to be considered for inclusion and adapted to specific contexts:

- Are they familiar with the elements of art?
- Have they been introduced to and understood a range of techniques?
- Are they conversant with a number of different relevant artists?
- Can they work independently?
- Are they willing to explore and experiment?
- Can they use their findings or experience?
- Have they got confidence?
- Have they got the ability to think in an open-ended way?
- Can they sequence?
- Can they make their own statements?

The scheme of work

Assessment, if it is to be effective, must be an integral part of the whole process of art education, neither dictating what is taught nor a meaningless 'bolt on' requirement. Rather it should be a means by which informed decisions can be made about the next step in the development of each child's art experience. Teaching and assessment go hand in hand and this is just as true for art as for any other area of the curriculum. It is particularly important that the unique nature of art education is understood both in respect to other subjects in the curriculum and in relation to art as a subject in its own right.

Clearly good organisation and planning are important. They show respect for the children and their work, and they affect children's learning experiences and the way in which we view them to assess them. An art programme where progression and development are clearly identified and set out for the whole school, although of paramount importance, is not easy to achieve in practice. The school art policy and scheme of work need to be debated

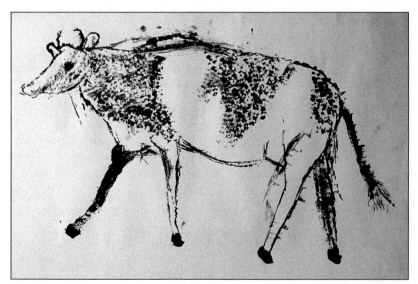

Cow. Print/drawing, 11 years. 33 x 23 cms

Horse chestnut. 13 years. 25 x 15 cms

and agreed upon by the whole staff. An ability to give leadership and examples of good practice in this matter is one of the important attributes of the art coordinator. A consistent approach throughout the school is vital for continuity of development and progression. Strategies for mixing paint, for example, should be established from the beginning, known and agreed upon by the whole staff, and consistently reinforced and developed.

It is understandable that some teachers are reluctant to create a rigid programme lest it should become a straightjacket which allows for no flexibility, thereby inhibiting the individual child's creative ideas and spontaneity. Assessment should not be so obvious and relentless that opportunities to be spontaneous and experimental are ignored. However, to allow a child always to proceed unhindered in art is to sidestep the rigours involved in identifying a clear and appropriate pathway, and could deny the child the opportunity to explore and develop the very knowledge and skills needed to make the next step forward or to express themselves more effectively. Differentiation, by which we mean the planning of work appropriate to the level of attainment and ability of each child, is also a key consideration, because assessment must take into account individual ability. If appropriate planning of the work is related to attainment targets, it will reveal whether the individual child has made progress. In this way assessment is not seen as a series of judgements on the child but a way of identifying how the child's art experience can be further developed. Clear objective criteria are the hallmark of perceptive teaching, where an understanding of a logical progression within the elements and techniques of art is coupled with an insight into the individual needs of children. An extreme interpretation of the requirement for assessment criteria can result in a rigid set of specific activities which follow relentlessly and without discrimination, culminating in a 'tick sheet'. The worst form of this is manifested in a series of worksheets which do not relate to first-hand experience or allow for creative and individual response. It is a holistic understanding of the structure which is important. A suggested range of 'vehicles' or activities might be very helpful to the non-specialist art teacher as long as they are seen for what they are – a selection of ideas which leave room for the class teacher to use professional judgement about detail and suitability or even their use at all in the context of other more relevant challenges.

A sensible balance is needed so that development can be promoted and children's enthusiasm harnessed and respected.

Recording

Many schools already have effective systems of recording in place but they need to be reviewed periodically in order that their efficiency can be scrutinised and questioned.

The recorded results of assessment should inform relevant parties about individual achievements in relation to stated objectives and should be formative as well as summative, providing a basis for further decisions about the shape of future learning. Teachers need also to assess their part in the process, as sometimes a child's inappropriate or inadequate response will result from the wrong task being set or the wrong questions being asked. A new analysis of the purpose of the task for a particular child will possibly result in the formulation of a more relevant or suitable approach. Recording the evidence allows for retrospective analysis to be applied and for informed discussion with a child, parent or previous teacher to take place. The records could also be used to modify and update the school's art policy-making into a cyclical process.

Reporting to parents, governors, colleagues

The task of reporting children's progress in art to pupils, their parents, governors and their subsequent teachers requires that there is a comprehensible language of art which is understood by all parties concerned so that true communication can take place. Parents and governors in particular need to be involved in aspects of art in the classroom so that there can be a mutual understanding of and respect for the art process. There should also be a dialogue between teachers so that there is a genuinely professional awareness of progress and development and a mutual understanding of the meaning of art education.

What is most important is that there is a consensus about what is of value in art and what constitutes evidence of that which is seen as valuable.

Evidence for assessment should include examples of both the process involved and the end product, and can be a combination of any of the following: images, artefacts, notebooks, work produced at home and tape-recorded discussions. These examples which can be selected alongside the child may be conveniently stored in a folder which has a pocket each side. This folder can provide evidence of experience and progression for teachers, parents and governors.

Folders showing work progression

2 Some different ways in which children work

SOME DIFFERENT
WAYS IN:
Focuses 1–5

There are many different ways of working, and it depends very much on each individual child as to the particular 'way in' which is found to be most effective.

Some children are very much more visually orientated than others and find that their strength is predominantly through looking at and interpreting first-hand experience, and they cannot have enough of it.

We should of course develop all children as far as we can down this particular avenue, but we must not forget that there are many children who function initially more strongly in other ways.

Victor Lowenfeld and Lambert Britten spoke of 'haptic' orientation where the dominant response to experience is through the sense of touch. He did not see it as only pertaining to the world of the blind or partially sighted. There is certainly quite a large number of children who seem to work experientially basing their imagery on a kind of symbolic knowledge well after the time when early symbolism leads many into visual realism. These children should of course be challenged to perceive, but we should be aware of the potential of their particular orientation. Very often, provided they are not discouraged, strong feeling for design, colour and decorative pattern can emerge and symbolism can develop into a valid and sophisticated mode of working provided paradoxically that it is fed richly on reality of all kinds, including the visual aspects.

In this section we suggest a variety of visual opportunities, and consider some ways in which children can be stimulated and challenged to work. The purpose for including a number of different ways of working is twofold. In the first place it underlines the fact that each individual calls upon different aspects of themselves and their experiences when undertaking work. Some as we have pointed out, are highly visually orientated, while others function more deeply from responding to feel. Thus we are extending the bases for working, and enabling them to come to terms with a wider range of possibilities which can show up strengths which could otherwise have been missed.

Second, different approaches can be an invaluable diagnostic tool for the teacher to gain insight into the children's strengths, orientation and needs, and to be able to assess their own input, vocabulary, and ways of teaching.

We have chosen five focuses which we believe cover a fairly broad spectrum. They pertain to imagery, visual perception, feeling/memory, personal involvement/ memory, and responding to artefacts.

Bicycle. Boy, 11 years. 17 x 23 cms

Focus 1: Imagery (p 31)

A drawing of yourself

(Direct drawing of a whole person with no preliminaries)

This challenge can be seen as a kind of 'control'.

A piece of work which is undertaken following an introduction which does not in fact give them any leads in regard to any visual or art element experience. This is in contrast to Focuses 2-5, which should offer interesting comparisons.

Tools/materials

A strong marking, dark drawing pencil; paper

Teacher introduction

A lively and encouraging challenge for the children to think about their own character, and what kind of person they are. Ask them to think about making a drawing to introduce themselves: what would they be wearing, or doing? Do not translate anything in the challenge into the language of art – the elements: line, tone, form, colour etc. – or how they would look.

Let the work take as long or as short a time as is necessary. Discuss the work.

The purpose of this drawing is to give some idea of the kind of imagery children present when not stimulated visually or through the senses.

Focus 2: Visual perception (pp 32-9)

A drawing of a child in profile sitting on a chair (from life)

Tools/materials

A strong marking, dark drawing pencil

Paper: *a* small piece for exploration of what kinds of marks can be made – dark/light, lines of varying thicknesses, solid tones, etc.

       b paper of the same kind for the drawing

The reason for setting up the model in profile is quite straightforward. The young child at the predominantly symbolist stage nearly always depicts the human figure in a full frontal position. In being confronted with this less usual aspect it is easy for the teacher to assess how much of the response is based on genuine perception. If the child is still completely symbolist, they will quite happily draw a full frontal figure. If the same kind of challenge is repeated at later dates it is very interesting to note developments in visually orientated perception. Young children who have moved into the latter mode invariably need longer to complete work, so plans need to be made to allow for this.

Teacher introduction

Immediately following the challenge to explore the potential of the pencil, discussion of the tool's potential needs to take place with all the pieces of work spread out on the floor or a low surface.

The model is then posed, and the challenge introduced. The children should be challenged to look and really see by every possible means, using a richly visual vocabulary and making them aware of character, pose, line, shade, pattern, texture, etc. General proportion might be mentioned, but on no account should 'rules' or 'measurement' be introduced at this stage. At least ten minutes should be spent on this introductory stimulus time for all but the youngest children.

The purpose of this challenge is to encourage children to work directly from visual perception. Whether we are successful or not depends on the words we use, how we introduce the subject, and on the point children have reached in the symbolist-realist continuum. It is important that we realise that intelligence is not necessarily synonymous with the visual realist approach. The work included over the following pages shows examples of work from a cross section of children who can be seen to have reached particular points on the continuum of symbolism/realism. To diagnose the point reached should help us to teach in ways relevant to their particular needs.

Some work by children with special educational needs is included among the examples. They fit into the continuum quite naturally, and as with children from mainstream schools we can never find a simplistic average for visual realism for a particular age group.

Girl, 6 years

Girl, 6 years

Girl, 8 years

Girl, 9 years

Boy, 9 years

Boy, 12 years

Note the stilted pose which is so often a characteristic of challenges where no lead is given in relation to visual or art element stimulus.

Most children of five years of age are largely symbolists. There will be some whose work is pre-figurative and some where visual realist clues are apparent. The children can look carefully and respond perceptively as in Nos 3 and 6. Others when looking at a figure in profile will revert to symbolism and draw a full frontal version as in No 1. The large head is typical of this stage for many children. In No 2 the round head is almost divided down the middle – a possible result of the profile challenge. The child is aware of 'furniture' but has not been able to seat the figure. No 4 has a nose in profile, but the eyes, the mouth, and possibly another nose or ear has been placed in the head shape. No 5 is an interesting mix of both modes. The placement of No 6 at the very edge of the paper was typical of a number of responses.

No 1 shows a profile head with one frontal eye and the other, which the child could just see, suggested by a mark inside the profile. In No 2 the drawing of the head shows a mixture of modes. The sitting position and the chair has been attempted and symbols have been used, including kneecaps. No 3 shows a mixture of frontal and profile aspects with both arms fully seen. Nos 5 and 6 are fully frontal. The symbol for the chair in No 5 is similar to the horseshoe shape of No 2. No 7 shows a strongly profiled approach with symbolist overtones, especially in the addition of the toes and the heel.

1

2a

b

3

4

5

6

At 7 years the children often fall between the modes of symbolist and visual realism. In Nos 5 and 6 the visual realist approach is apparent. No 1 shows half a face in a frontal head in response to the profile challenge. In Nos 2 (a) and (b) (by the same girl), the figure has been more successfully related to the chair in (b) but there is less interest in the profile. No 4 shows a full face with the profile drawn within it. There are a number of visual realist clues in No 3 together with the symbolist's large head and the eye right at the front. The pattern of the fingers has been enjoyed to the forgetfulness of actual numbers (this is not uncommon). There is less interest in detail and more symbolism as the child moves down the figure.

By 8 years many children have moved into a visual realist mode or their symbolism is being informed by it. No 1 is an example of the latter: a large headed figure with hair added, and a profile showing keen interest in the ear, nostril, lips and teeth. The eye is presented in detail and is a full frontal view in the profile head. (The early Egyptians used this particular mode of symbolism.) Nos 2 and 5 show a firmly visual realist approach including the eyes seen in profile. No 3 is moving into the visual realist realm. Note the adjustment in the drawing of the hand. Nos 4(a) and (b) are by the same child. The orientation is visual realist. The placement of the eyes at the very front of the head is not unusual, and has symbolist roots – you *know* in a feeling way that your eye is 'in front'.

All of these drawings show evidence of visual realist orientation, even No 2(a) with the exception of the head. Clearly some teaching challenge to look at shape and line had gone on before this same child tackled No 2(b). No 1 has symbolist overtones, showing a profile head with the body swung round to the unseen frontal view. There is an enjoyment of character in this drawing. The chair is in profile. This, and No 2(b) have proportionally large heads. The other four drawings on the page show a greater awareness of proportion. No 3 shows a more mature approach as the figure is sketched and strengthened into a holistically seen pose. Nos 5(a) and (b) are by the same boy. There is a difference in the quality of looking in No 5(b) on the evidence of the drawing of the head, and body shapes and lines.

1

2

3

4

5

6

There is evidence of a basic orientation toward the visually real in these examples together with interest in the details of hands and faces. There will still be some exceptions at this age. The proportion of the head still tends to be large in some drawings and Nos 2 and 4 show that the children were having problems with relationship of arm to body proportions. There is an overall 'feel' for the general poses. No 4 shows a profile with two eyes, which is a symbolist approach, and the legs are in the same orientation. Shadows are shown cast by the chair legs. No 5 has a frontal eye in a profile head. Nos 5 and 6 show an awareness of solid form through the use of tone and line.

1

2a

2b

3

4

5

6

The symbolist orientation is still apparent in Nos 2(b) and 3. In No 2(a) an attempt has been made to look, but the problems of relationship and shape are too great for this boy, and the second attempt places the figure from memory or expectation in a frontal pose. In No 3 the problems of a visual realist/symbolist mix is shown with a frontal eye, head shape with interior nose, and body swung round to frontal position. No 1 shows a generalised figure with detailed trainers. Nos 4, 5 and 6 show a visual realist orientation. In many cases we found that the trainers were detailed and the make named.

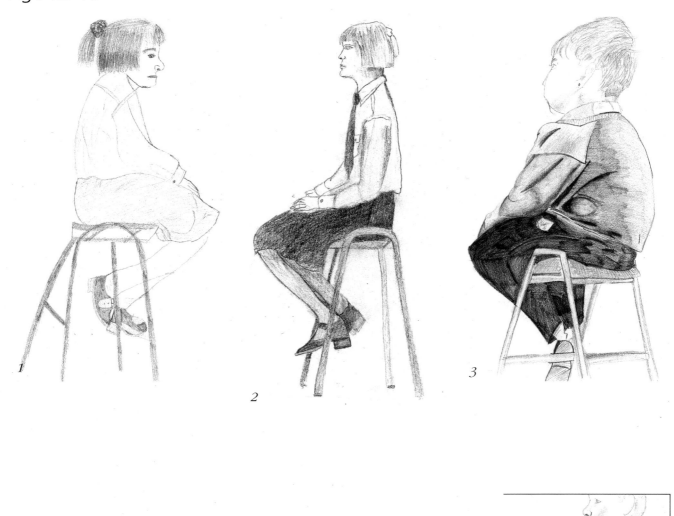

At this age there is a much more general interest in character and the feeling of the way the body is positioned. Form plays an important role and is described through the use of tone and line. There will always be a number of children who when attempting visual realist drawings bring symbolist approaches to the challenge. There is evidence of the head proportion being large in relation to the body in Nos 3, 4 and 6. In No 4 in particular the desire has been to get the whole figure on the page regardless of proportional relationships. Nos 5 and 6 have a more mature visual realist approach where the children have been content to leave the legs partly unfinished (5) or to draw part of the head cut by the top of the paper (6).

Focus 3: Feeling and memory (pp 42-3)

A drawing of someone to whom the child is related by warmth of feeling (family or friend)

The feeling response can sometimes break barriers in an interesting way which some children find difficult in a memory challenge, or even in visual perception. Memory/feeling work can be an excellent use of the sketchbook at home. These challenges depend entirely on the ability of the teacher to trigger memory by means of colourful use of visual words.

Tools/materials

Coloured graphic tools of a wide variety or strong dark mark-making pencils

Paper   *a*   small pieces for exploration work with the tools

       b   larger pieces of the same kind for the drawing

Teacher introduction

1 Having organised the graphic tools and smaller piece of paper the children can be challenged to explore and experiment covering the surface with everything the tools can do – including overlaying. Spread work onto floor or low surface and discuss the effects.

2 Immediately afterwards ask the children to think of someone they know well and are fond of. Lead them through a series of trigger points to help them to visualise the person standing or sitting close to them (asking children to close their eyes to imagine them often helps).

Do not encourage the children to discuss for this particular challenge, as the aim is to get each individual to build up their own picture, and other children's ideas do not help this process.

'Is your person standing or sitting or in some other position?'

'What expression is on their face – Happy? Friendly? Sad?…'

'Is the face lined or smooth? – picture it.'

'What is the hair like? – straight? Curling? Short? Long? or has your person a bald head?'

'What colour is the hair? Black? Brown? Fair? Ginger? White? Grey? or some other colour?

'What are they wearing? What does the surface feel like?'

'Is the clothing patterned? What kind of a pattern?'

'What really shows the character of the person? Is it their expression? The way they stand or sit? The colours they wear?'

'Do you think they are 'warm' people or 'cold' people ?'

'Show me what you think in your drawing.'

This is an example of open-ended triggering which can be developed in many different ways and circumstances. Let the work take its own time.

Discuss the work and what has happened.

The purpose of this work is to assess the child's use and need of an involved or feeling response. Part of the result will also depend on the quality of the teacher involvement and trigger descriptions.

Focus 4: Personal involvement/memory (pp 44-5)

A drawing and/or model of themselves having experienced some kind of movement or drama involvement immediately prior to the work

This could be any aspect of physical education, swimming, dance or any kind of drama. The examples we have chosen are based on drama and movement.

Tools/materials

Drawing tools – chalk, charcoal, or hoghair brushes and black paint mixed to a thick ink-like consistency.

Mid-toned, neutral coloured sugar paper, large and of varying shape and/or clay of appropriate consistency for hand modelling. (Each child to have a ball of clay which can be cupped in the hands.)

Teacher introduction

Before the challenge build up a safe construction of tables and chairs into shapes which when covered with blankets, tarpaulins etc. form a sequence of tunnels or caves, just large enough for children to crawl through. Introduce the idea of exploring caves and with children working in pairs, or threes, offer each group the use of a small torch or bicycle lamp

Build up the dramatic experience, triggering atmosphere by discussion of sights, sounds, smells and feeling – imagine touching the surfaces: are they warm? Cold? Wet? Dry? Imagine the darkness and small amount of light, the dripping sounds, or water rushing in the distance, the smell of mould or water. Build up these experiences through discussion, involving the children deeply. How would they feel? Afraid? Excited? This can develop into story sequences or each small group with torch on can move slowly and carefully through the constructed cave, and then back.

Following this experience each child may choose a piece of paper and drawing tools/materials, or a ball of clay. The work should be undertaken in reasonable space to allow for strong gestural drawings – standing at tables or desks, or working on the floor. The challenge will be for the children to make a drawing or model of themselves in the cave/tunnel and to communicate how it might feel.

Children may well wish to undertake a series of pieces of work rather than one only, and this is to be encouraged.

Discuss the work and what has happened.

The purpose of this challenge is to involve children in a personal experience or feeling response, and to assess the strengths of this particular kind of approach. Does the work show different qualities to the observational work, and if so in what way?

8 years

7 years

7 years

8 years

8 years

8 years

a 9 years   *b 9 years*

a 9 years   *b 9 years, 'The best thing I've ever done'*

a 12 years   *b 12 years*

FOCUS 4

Children moving and drawing,
5 years

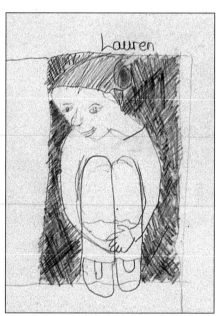

Children using
boxes to experience
and draw

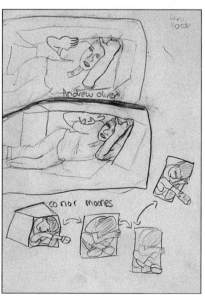

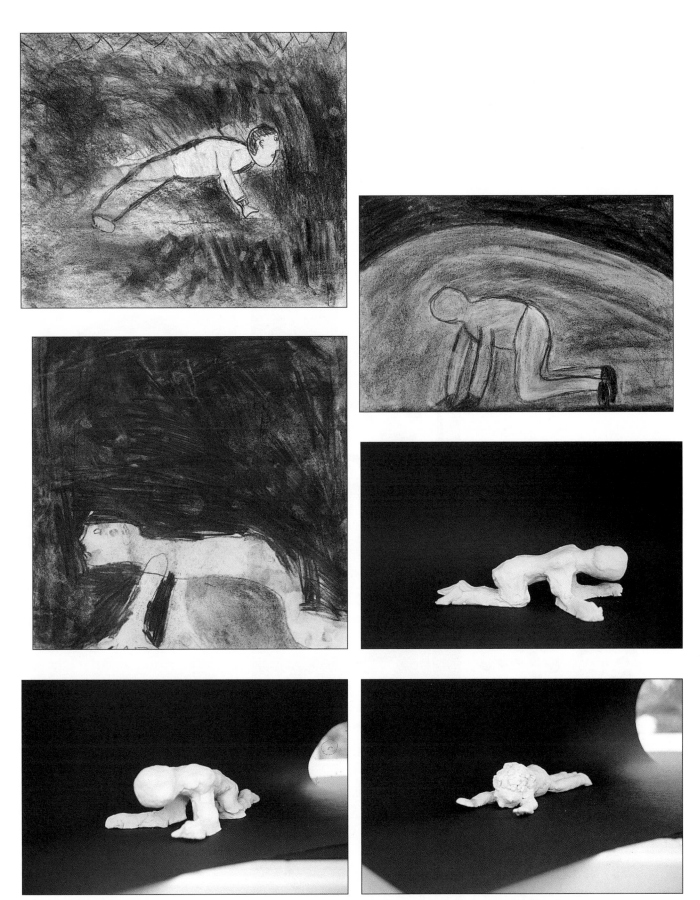

Children drawing, and modelling in clay following experience of a dark constructed 'tunnel', 9 years

FOCUS 5: Responding to artefacts (p 48)

A five year old at work

After looking at T.C. Cannon's painting 'Caddo Kiawa' (His hair flows like a river) – A North American Indian portrait

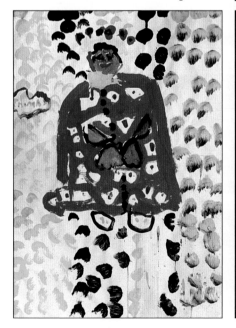

Boy in a top hat, 9 years

*After Cannon's 'Caddo
Kiawa', 9 years*

*After Picasso's
'Young woman
looking in a
mirror', 9 years*

47

Focus 5: Responding to artefacts (pp 46-51)

A portrait painting of a character after looking at and discussing the work of a number of artists

Ideally we would be working from originals. However, in this classroom project we used reproductions selected from our personal collections, which included gallery prints, cuttings from books, magazines and calendars. These were mounted and displayed in a mini gallery arrangement.

Resources/tools/materials

We have chosen nine reproductions of portrait paintings of people wearing a hat or headgear. These range from the Renaissance to the Twentieth Century, and are depicted in frontal, three-quarter, or profile positions. A variety of approaches, strong use of media, interesting colour and shape were the criteria for choice.

A model or models will be needed to wear some kind of hat and costume, to be set in front of a backdrop of coloured or dark cloth (plain material).

Powder, liquid tempera, or acrylic paint. It is important to work in the kinds of paint which can be used thickly and expressively. The children will need to have explored and experiemented with paint and know something of the variety of effects they could achieve.

Hoghair brushes of varying size.

Good quality sugar or cartridge paper of varying sizes and shapes.

White or coloured chalk. Pencils are not recommended for drafting in this instance as the image often becomes too tight, restricted and detailed to handle as a basis of 'painterly' paintings.

Boards or surfaces to work on. It is important to ensure that children are able to position themselves at a reasonable distance from their work rather than in a writer's position, which is too close to appraise a painting. To stand, or to kneel on a chair or use an easel is preferable. Some children need to be encouraged to work in this way.

Teacher input

Prepare materials and arrange the room for the model or models to be positioned in front of the cloth backdrop/s.

Gather the children around the 'mini gallery' and encourage discussion. Use the strengths of the moment but introduce the following:

Why do people paint portraits?

Are portraits always lifelike, or like photographs?

What are these painters trying to tell us about the people they are painting? Do we get some kind of feeling from them?

Has colour been used to give special effects? (Shape, line, pattern, tone, texture etc. could also be introduced here.)

How has the paint been put on?

What kind of tools do you think might have been used?

Build up a series of questions which lead children to make judgements which require different criteria:

- Which painting do you like best?
- Which painting do you think is the most lifelike?
- What can we know about this person?
- Which artist has given you the strongest feeling of what the person was like?
- Which artist has used colour to tell us something about the sitter? How? (The same question could apply to the other elements – shape, pattern, line, tone etc.)
- Which person looks the happiest, saddest, sternest, youngest, oldest (based on the particular selection)?

- How has the painter given you this impression?
- Have you changed your mind about the one you like?

The point which soon becomes clear in an exercise of this sort is that depending on the question, different paintings are chosen as being the most successful, or in the young child's terms 'the best'. The whole question/discussion session can be an excellent educational language experience too.

After the discussion and when the model/s are set in front of the draped background, the children can be introduced to the idea of painting a half-length, or head and shoulders portrait as large as they can make it on the chosen piece of paper.

The idea is to think of the sitter as any kind of person they would wish, in that position, and wearing that particular hat. What kind of person can they imagine wearing it? They could be young or old, happy, sad, kindly, stern, whatever they wish.

The portrait can be painted in the manner of any of the works they have been looking at, and the real colours of the model in front of them, including the background, can be changed to help them to say something about the chosen character. The model is there to help the children to look, and is useful for the teacher to talk about ways in which the hat fits the head, the way the hair shows, the shape of the face and the features they can see. Encourage them to look at the way the head is held by the neck, and how the shoulders look from where they are working. Real perception is the aim, and this can be undermined when rigid formulae, measurement and so-called rules of proportion are enforced.

The purpose of this challenge is to give the children insight into the ways in which artists work, and to enable them to realise that they too can work in part from observation, but with the ability to change and use elements in order to convey their own meaning.

Reflection

If some or all of these focuses have been put into practice it is interesting to look at the results both at a class or group level, and at an individual level. Of course the first thing which will need appraising is the actual way we communicated with the children, the tools and materials we provided. Following this we will need to learn from what has been done:

Group: Were some modes of working more successful than others? Which ways of working caused the most insightful imagery? Which ways of working caused the richest element response?

Individual: Were individuals more able to respond strongly in some focuses than in others? Which focuses were particular children orientated with?

An important issue for the future will be to ask the question as to whether this experience might broaden or change the way in which we couch future challenges, for the whole class, groups, or individuals.

Discussion with the children as to the different strengths and weaknesses in their opinion of the different ways of working is a very enlightening exercise.

Boy, 9 years

'I painted Thomas in a top hat. I chose Picasso's painting of a young woman because it had bright colours like red and yellow and pretty tessellated patterns. The lady was beautiful on the outside but wasn't kind, so was ugly on the inside and it shows in the reflection.

It was difficult doing the painting, but it was fun.'

Girl, 9 years

'I decided to do the painting of the man in the fox hat (TC Cannon) because it was a spectacular painting. I like it because it had lots of bright colours. The painting meant to me, the man was supposed to be quite stubborn. The Otto Dix 'Café Couple' gave me the creeps.

I found the painting difficult to paint but I enjoyed it very much.'

Girl, 9 years

'I chose the painting 'His hair flows like a river' because it's full of thick bright colours and big shapes. It stands out and looks spectacular hung on the wall.

I chose Thomas for my model because he can sit still, and I liked the top hat he wore. I started with the big shapes and then I put in the details. I found that it was easy to paint Thomas quickly but well, but the background was very time-consuming. If I did another one I would choose Vanessa Bell's 'Spanish Lady' because I love the way she has her veil and the lovely red dress.'

After Cannon's 'Caddo Kiawa (His Hair Flows Like a River)'

After Modigliani. 7 years

After Vanessa Bell's 'Self portrait'. 9 years

After Van Gogh's 'Old Peasant'. 12 years

After Roualt's 'Old King'. 12 years

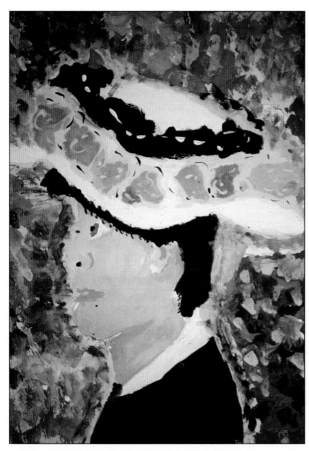

After Vanessa Bell's 'Self Portrait'. 12 years

After Francesco Foscari. 12 years

SKETCHBOOKS: PERSONAL CELEBRATION AND RESEARCH

Sketchbooks in the development of the child

Many artists in the past, notably Constable, Turner, Van Gogh, Picasso and Henry Moore, have used sketchbooks as a tool in a number of different ways: for gathering information, practising drawing skills, experimenting and working out ideas. Although it has to be acknowledged that not all artists work in this way, there is a significant number for whom currently the sketchbook is vital – for example David Hockney, Anthony Green and Rachel Whiteread. It is important that children experience at first hand this fundamental tool of the artist and through working in this way develop a sense of being part of this artistic tradition.

A number of artist's sketchbooks are published in replica and these can offer opportunities to gain insight into the functions of a sketchbook, and how it is influenced by the owner's intentions and experiences. Additionally it can be arranged for teachers and/or pupils from the local senior school to visit with their sketchbooks, and occasionally it is discovered that there is a parent in the school who habitually uses one.

Sketchbooks have an important role to play in the development of self-esteem, particularly where they include items of personal interest and drawings of things that surround them, as well as an opportunity to work from imagination and fantasy.

If children are given encouragement and the right environment in which to use sketchbooks, where they are allowed time for reflection on gathered material and ideas, and for the development of an image over a period of time, then they help to eliminate unnecessary feelings of anxiety about drawing which often accompany the expectation of the immediate production of a finished piece. By allowing the child to plan work properly and proceed when the time is right for them the task is also given value.

In schools planning schedules are tight but there are occasions when, in order to experiment and explore, to make rough drafts, develop ideas and produce quality work, children need time. Sadly it is seldom that we say to a child 'I don't mind how long you take'.

Where sketchbooks become a familiar tool and a regular way of working, they can, by developing a systematic and gradual organisation of skills, change a child's attitude to learning. Through the collection and selection of materials children develop an awareness of the value of process in relation to the finished piece. Where they are encouraged to be autonomous, to test out ideas, to experiment and to plan, the sketchbook can be a means whereby these elementary research skills are fostered; and this can prove relevant to other areas than art experience.

Sketchbooks are also an arena where discussion can take place, using the language and vocabulary of art. This exercising of an emergent art vocabulary helps to develop and articulate a growing understanding of what it is to appreciate and make art, and encourages powers of discrimination and critical analysis. As well as stimulating the child's comments and observations this can also be an opportunity to offer positive help, for example by enabling the child to look in a particular way while drawing from the figure, focusing children through comments such as 'look at the shape of the shoulders', 'what kind of line are you going to use to describe the way she is sitting?' It is important for the teacher also to develop a vocabulary so that appropriate questions can be asked.

Sometimes the comment 'I don't mind how much experimenting you do' is a most important part of the conversation, and the most valuable outcome is to let the child know that he or she can have another chance, and another. Drawing, like writing, needs a number of attempts.

It is important that children begin to learn how to assess their work. Following a challenge the children could be invited to analyse what they have done and learned, the teacher's response being one of positive encouragement and advice rather than negative criticism. Although for some there is a perceived mismatch between a declaration that a sketchbook is a personal document and an intention to make comments in it, this dichotomy can be overcome if the situation is handled with respect and sensitivity.

The developing sketchbook

It is very useful for children sometimes to make their own sketchbooks as this increases the feeling of ownership. However, successful books can be created from a standard exercise book with plain pages fixed into a cover which has been made and personalised by the child.

Sketchbooks are a vital tool for young children from the very beginning of schooling. They can be introduced from reception where they are likely to be a combination of 'newsbook', a book for testing out/playing with materials and a space in which children can draw freely.

Initially young children will benefit from a sketchbook which is quite large in format, and which will allow for expressive experiment as well as some more delicate observational work. This often means that the book has a soft cover the same size as the pages, the two being secured by a big stitch through the middle. The type of sketchbook should change and grow with the child's developing needs, experience and expertise, and the purpose of the book.

As children get older they realise that they will need different sketchbooks for different purposes. A variety of methods of making a sketchbook can be offered, including some more complex. For example one with hard covers could be made or one containing a variety of different kinds of paper. Increasing responsibility should be given to the child for deciding on the size, type of paper and format of the sketchbook, and when to use it.

Following their investigations into the seven sketchbooks of Vincent Van Gogh, one class of nine and ten year olds designed and made their own covers with accessories. They discovered that he constructed his own books, some of which had a storage compartment or even a pencil holder. They further personalised their books by giving them names.

Often a standard style of book is provided by the time children reach secondary school. One teacher who used plain exercise books supplied by the school bound two consecutive books together so that both children and teacher could refer back to previous ideas. From the front each book contained work initiated in the classroom, while the back of the book was used for work done at home. Individuality and the feeling of ownership was not lost. Children could still choose to personalise the cover in their own time.

Sketchbook covers

53

Observational drawing of tadpoles. 5 years

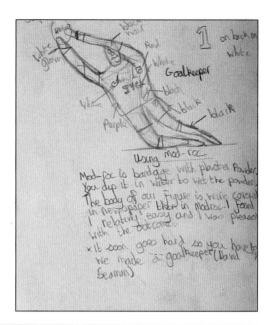

Preparatory work for project on movement

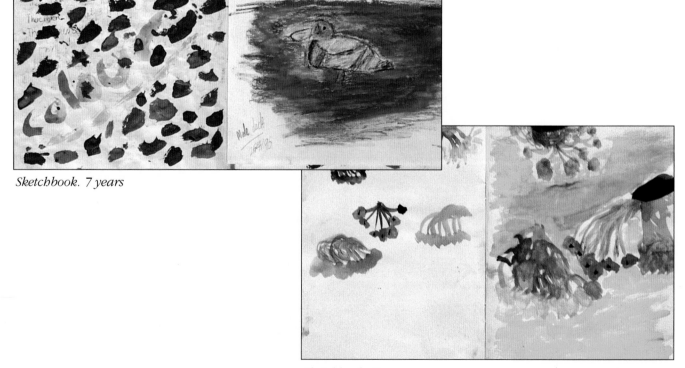

Sketchbook. 7 years

Sketchbook. 7 years

Exploring line and tone. 10 years

Portrait: Initial exploration of features. 11 years

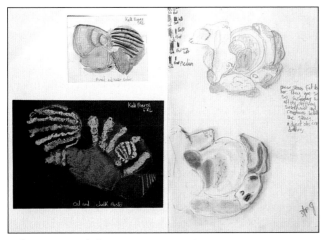

Observational drawing: Form. 10 years

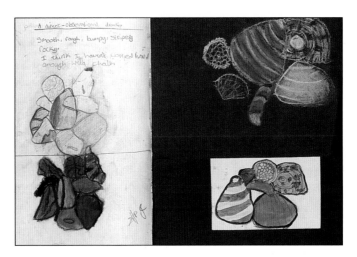

Observational drawing: Still life (set up by the children).
12 years

Sketchbooks in the development of the task

Art experience develops in many ways, through spontaneous drawing, play and experiment, and through the investigation of materials to find out how they work. At first the experience of 'playing with materials' is similar to the experience of babies experimenting with language and sound, and consequently is often a random activity. Alongside this it is useful to develop a methodology so that by purposeful experiment, focused information gathering, informed development of ideas and systematic analysis of a process, sketchbooks become a way of structuring learning. The teacher can observe the child's natural inclinations and preferences but also offer an opportunity for guided exploration and experiment similar to a warming-up activity. An example of this would be experimental mark-making in the sketchbook, using a selection of materials in order to explore their potential before embarking on a related piece of work. It is important that the material experimented with is one which is to be used in the final drawing and that the child understands that the reason for experimenting first is so that an informed decision can be made about which is the most appropriate material or tool for the job.

It is sometimes necessary for the teacher to build in an element of constraint so that the task, although experimental, can remain controlled and focused. For example the range of tools can be limited, and in a colour investigation the colours made available can initially be limited to one or two primaries and either black or white and the task structured so that the children have a methodology for organising the results. As a sketchbook methodology develops and becomes familiar, the children will become more autonomous in restricting their materials and structuring their own investigations.

'Having something to say', the quality of the image, and its development, are areas which are a challenge and can sometimes be neglected or missed altogether. A sketchbook can provide a place for the collection of a variety of reference material to inspire, stimulate imagination, and to inform and enrich the end result, for example a collection of drawings around a theme as a learning experience both in its own right and because it provides a collection of images to select from. It is not merely a starting point but a place to return to for further development and inspiration.

In order for the contents of a sketchbook to be stimulating and exciting, they need to come from a variety of sources – for example drawing visits to farm parks, museums and galleries. Children can take their sketchbooks into movement or dance lessons and draw each other or themselves as they felt when

Museum studies. 7 years

56

they were moving. Experimental pieces of weaving, texture or batik can also be stored and annotated with details of the process. Materials for inclusion which have the potential to initiate, support and extend work should include examples which relate to the child's own ideas and interests. Postcards and cuttings can be put in. Visitors to the school can provide another source, particularly if they bring stimulating visual material with them. Older children, students or staff showing or lending their sketchbooks can help to stimulate their broader use and show the personal nature of some of the imagery. Nothing can take the place of seeing original sketchbooks.

We have seen that through developing tasks which are identifiable and practised, certain constants and basic skills will be rehearsed through continuous use of the sketchbook. In addition there will be the consolidation of knowledge gained from learning about artists. There is often evidence of play and experimentation. However there has to be a stage where these things serve to inform the development of ideas, and a time when the teacher leads individuals on to to explore alternative solutions from which they will choose to say something further, possibly but not inevitably through the production of a finished piece of work.

A well-managed sketchbook also provides evidence for assessment and pointers for future work, so that it is not just a starting point but a place to return to to solve intermediate problems and to gain inspiration in a cycle of development. It is possible to be blinkered in looking for a specific outcome in art and consequently to miss important aspects of the child's development. For this and many other reasons it is valuable to sit with the child and to talk about what they feel has gone on in the sketchbook. In order to be able to communicate purposefully, both teacher and child should develop a mutually understood vocabulary relating to art and the particular task in hand.

One way to build this vocabulary is through the discussion which introduces children to a challenge and starts to prepare them for it. An annotated sketchbook in which tasks are broken down into a sequence is another way. This can increasingly become the responsibility of the child and can form a basis for self-assessment. For example if the challenge was one relating to colour mixing, the work can be assessed by asking questions similar to the following: Can you make six tints and tones of yellow? Can you use the six yellows to paint a vase of flowers? Can you mix other colours?

From the evidence which the sketchbook offers – experiments, collections of factual and inspirational material, analysis of methods, annotations and embryos of ideas – there is an opportunity for the teacher to get to know the child as an individual and see how they have progressed. Looking back with the child through the contents of sketchbooks is a way of looking at what they have actually done and through discussion gain insight into the decisions that have been made, the thought that has been behind those decisions, and the learning which has taken place.

Test pieces: String block print dyed surface. 11 years

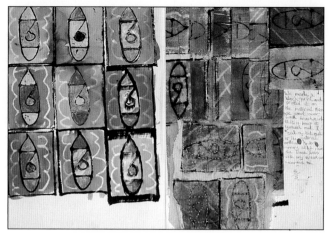

Developing pattern and line into wax resist. 12 years

Recording from researched information. 10 years

Exploration of texture and collage. 12 years

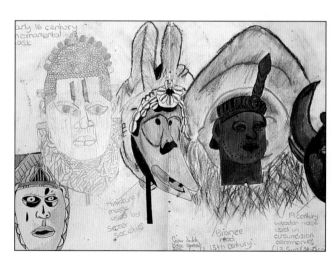

Art from other cultures to develop into batik and print. 13 years

Art from another culture: Aztec pattern developed from researched ideas.
10 years

Exploring colour from magazine fragment and relating it to the work of Howard Hodgkin and Patrick Heron.
12 years

A small chosen image developed in a wide variety of materials. 10 years

3 The ways of the teacher

David Downes, 4 years

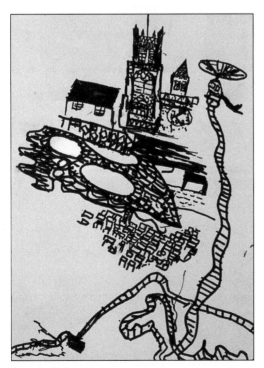

David Downes, 6 years

Art is unique. It is not only non-verbal, it is pre-verbal. It deals with visual and tactile learning, response, communication and expression in ways in which no other areas of the curriculum do. It is a mixture and balance of logical and intuitive experience presented in a visual and tactile way. It is clearly, although of course not solely, a highly intellectual educational pursuit, and it can use all the ways of working a human being is capable of.

The teacher holds a privileged responsibility to use art and facilitate it in its fullest sense, and it is appropriate to consider what it takes to engage the child to function and develop fully in the discipline.

In the first place we need to consider ourselves as teachers, and think what we want from the children. Hopefully we shall come to the conclusion that we want each child to be involved in personal work which continually builds and deepens experience of the nature and language of art and design, and enables each one to have the autonomy and interest to move forward after our own support is withdrawn. Surely the real mark of success is what happens when our children move on from us. We need all through our teaching life to appraise our preconceptions. Are we really right in presupposing what our particular children can handle or are good at? For example, many of us have been surprised at children's concentration spans when introduced to particular stimuli. This has often been noted when artists work in schools, or children respond to artefacts or other interesting items (ordinary though they may be) through first-hand experience. Another example is based on a taught preconception of some years ago in teacher education. This stated that young children should only be given *big* brushes, and *big* sheets of paper. We now know that although some children respond wonderfully to this stimulus, it is only part of the picture, and some children are worried and frustrated by a continual expectation of this kind. Certainly children should be challenged and encouraged to work in this way, but they should also be challenged to work with graphic tools which offer the opportunity for detail and precision, and small scale. The example of David Downes, who became really frustrated and upset when faced with large work, but came to life when introduced to biros and fibre tips, is interesting in this context.

The worrying thing is that our expectations can often cause our prophesies to be fulfilled. Children learn to give us very much what they think we want at every level. What do they think we want should be our interest throughout, and conversation with children can lead us to a greater understanding of what they really think and are aiming at.

The second aspect of the teaching challenge is the provision of an appropriate working and learning environment, and good quality tools and materials. These aspects should be seen for what they are – overt teaching requirements, and they set the scene for the quality or lack of it in the work that the children produce.

The environment is a whole-school matter as well as being pertinent to each class teacher, and should be a place of interest and order where children can feel sufficiently secure to involve themselves in study and research, practical work or relaxation. Our organisation for the resources and our rooms, preparing for lessons and clearing away should of course be exemplary. There is a need for resources of all kinds of first-hand stimuli, and it is sensible to consider this problem at a whole-school level. The lucky minority have been able to turn a spare room into a 'museum', but others have recesses, parts of corridors and classrooms for the purpose. Happily all the exhibits are never in the base together as there is a continual programme of usage. Loans from parents, staff, local industries and businesses and local authority loan schemes augment these collections. They should play a major role in our teaching, and so are vital to our needs. Materials and tools are also of crucial importance, and we should never expect children to use poor quality instruments and media which we ourselves would find it difficult to function with. Basic tools and materials for drawing, painting, printing, textiles and three-dimensional work (including a good basic clay) are everyday requirements.

The minimum colour range necessary for paint is to have black and white, and warm and cold reds, yellows and blues. Anything less does not give children a full mixing range. The quality of pigment is important and should allow for strong opaque usage. Powder and liquid tempera colour are excellent (solid tempera discs are not recommended because of their poor covering quality and wear on brushes).

There is a need for an ever-growing bank of original artefacts and reproductions for everyday use. Originals can be displayed around the school and in classrooms. Reproductions can be in the form of books, cuttings, postcards and gallery prints, and can be stored in folders, box files and manilla envelope files. The class and school library is an appropriate place for storing these. Without consideration of the place and the means of working, even the best methods of teaching are doomed to failure.

African head. Girl, 13 years

FLOWERS

—

Flowers and plants can be a wonderful resource and stimulus for working and can be used in many ways. These can range from botanical drawings to rich paintings and three-dimensional work.

These examples show a series of paintings, some of which have been enhanced by the children studying the work of Gustav Klimt, Georgia O'Keefe or David Hockney. It is important when stimulating painting subjects to take into account the whole picture surface – the group and what can be seen around it. The flower border paintings looked after themselves with attention drawn to the earth and surrounding plants, but the flowers and receptacles often need some kind of drape or paper behind them, or to be placed in a window. So-called imagined background painted in before or after the flower painting often weakens the work as the tones, colours, contrasts and similarities cannot be seen as an integral whole.

Vase of flowers. 30 x 15 cms. Press print, 10 years

Flower border after looking at Gustav Klimt painting

Flowers and interior. 50 x 47 cms, 10 years

Bowl of flowers and snail. 9 years

Flower painting after looking at David Hockney painting

Flowers.
60 x 47 cms.
10 years

Flowers and
spotted
background.
55 x 47 cms.
8 years

Flowers in a
glass jar.
30 x 25 cms.
12 years

Tulip head, after
looking at Georgia
O'Keefe paintings

Flower head, after looking at Georgia O'Keefe
paintings

Iris in a glass jar.
27 x 16 cms.
Boy, 11 years

LIGHTING-UP TIME

Our teaching began with our room organisation, appropriate first hand stimuli and material resources. Next, the initial energy to begin the project needs careful consideration. The strength of good teaching has always been to internalise whatever challenge we are setting in the child's experience. It is not a subject 'out there', it is a bit of life experience within you. If art teaching is worth its salt it literally changes the way we see things, for after we look we understand more, and we realise there is still to come more to understand. It also changes the way in which we work, building up more confidence in our way of making tools and materials, teaching us through exploration, experimentation and usage. 'I could try this, – or this' is music to a teacher's ears.

Clearly whether we are successful or not depends on our stimuli, materials and organisation, but having put these in place we can think of no better description than Tim Wilson's when he speaks of the need for a 'lighting-up time'. It is what you show and, how you show it, what you say and, how you say it, and what children say in response and discussion. It is how we engage

Tonal head study. Boy, 13 years

64

children in the living experience of the challenge, it is a build-up of creative force and energy before the actual creative work is undertaken. It is not just a matter of confronting children with a stimulus, be it materials, an item, an experience, a poem or a visit to a place, however interesting, which causes education to happen, but it is the way in which it is introduced – the 'lighting-up time'. This is so basic that many teachers already know it, but for the inexperienced teacher it is of crucial importance.

To start with we need to see the potential of our children, and of the art experience we introduce to them. Our own enthusiasm is a vital ingredient in the drama, and we can all think of examples of exactly the same words from two different people having totally different impacts and messages. What it comes to in the end is not only our words, but the way in which we say them.

Whether we are introducing an item, a happening or some verbal stimulus like a poem we need to use words creatively. Language which uses visual and tactile response offers a sure footing for beginning. It enables a deeper level of perception and offers a different level of recall or creation of imagery. It is well worth experimenting with different approaches to find what is most effective. If the power of the imagery and the vocabulary used is steadily built up, children's response in discussion can deepen. There is a point however, which the experienced teacher will know is the optimum time for the practical challenge to take place, and with enthusiasm and energy running high work begins. The length of time given to this initial teaching could well benefit from taking up to a quarter of the lesson. Strongly motivated children will cover more ground in the remaining time than less interested children will cover in the whole time.

INTERACTION

The interaction between teacher and child during the practical part of the lesson plays a major role in teaching, and it is as important to know when to leave children alone as to know when to talk to them. As teachers we have to define parameters within which to enable our children to have personal choice. Clearly there is always a need to listen to children's intentions rather than to take our own interpretations for granted – it is surprising how many times one can be wrong! It is also very important to build up a mutually understood vocabulary to enable real communication to take place. We must realise that what is happening is living and growing, and may need us to deviate from our original intentions if real and effective learning is to go on. Different but equally valid goals may be being achieved, and we should be flexible.

The key question in the teacher's mind must be where the work needs to be taken next. The child may well know, and be allowed to get on with it, but there may be opportunities to point out what has been done, positively or by sensitive questioning, or by suggestions to lead them to think of other possibilities or choices. This is on-going practical negotiated assessment at its best. Teacher input will include individual tutorial, or class tutorial when a general teaching point is to be made.

CULMINATION

If work is not completed in one session it is very likely that a second 'lighting-up time' is beneficial at the beginning of the next session in order to focus children's minds and energies afresh. It is more than likely too that new teaching points have arisen from the on-going work, or that the challenge itself calls for new inputs.

As projects are finished it is important to maximise the educational potential. In the first place the way in which we receive and keep work gives children a very strong message as to our consideration of its value. In the second place lies the whole area of how we are going to communicate to children what they have done, its value, and the things it might lead to. It is important too to celebrate what has been done, and to share the pleasure of achievement.

⟶ p 68

NATURAL OBJECTS

The children were introduced to a variety of natural objects including shells, feathers and snakeskin. Richly visual word descriptions were included as the children looked at the stimuli. The class was challenged to discuss and investigate the items before making analytical drawings

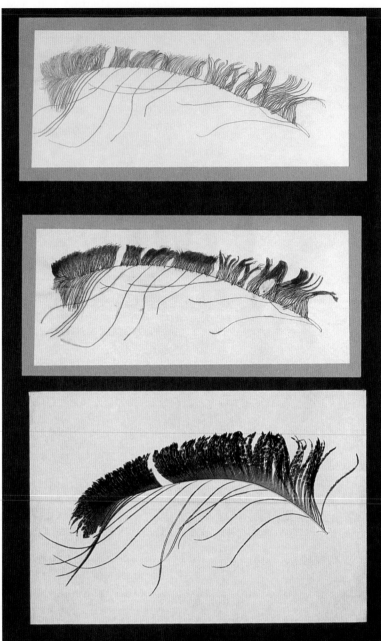

(Above and opposite) *Analytical drawings of natural objects 9-11 years*

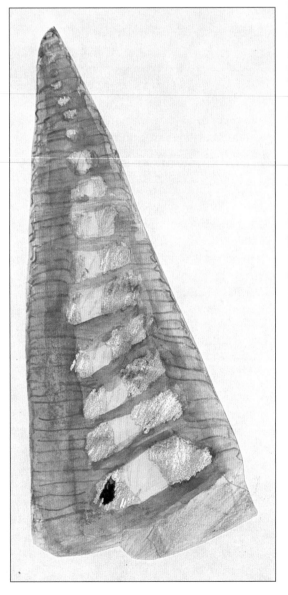

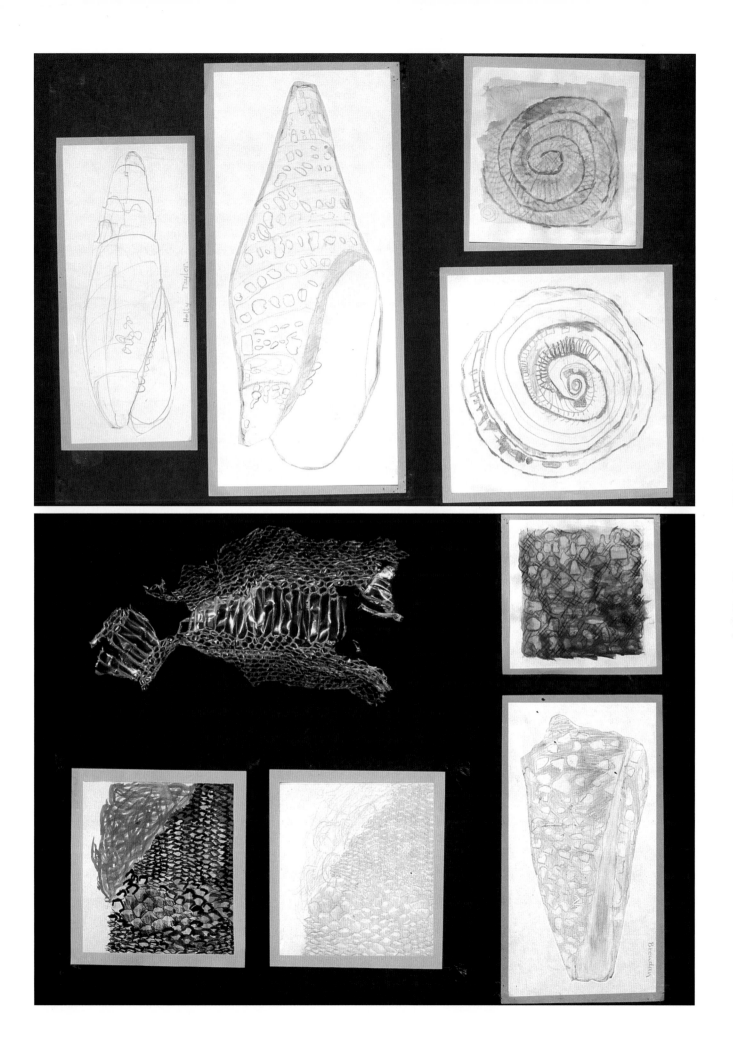

Children should be enabled to view and discuss their work in order to understand what has been achieved. A very useful and quick way to enable this is by means of a 'pavement show' where the work is spread out in a carefully spaced manner on a floor in a classroom, hall or corridor. For best effect each piece or group of pieces can be placed on a neutral backing paper. This is a realistic way of distancing children to enable them to see and discuss what has been done, and of showing all the work, including exploration and experimentation, in context.

No doubt a selection of work relevant to children's and teaching needs is displayed in classrooms or elsewhere. All children need encouragement, but to put work up without giving the reason why can be embarassing for some. That it was his or her 'best effort' can be a misery if the rest of the class are insensitively judgmental. Some quality of the work needs to be focused on, and this is not difficult in practice. Strong use of a particular element of art rather than overall imagery and content really does leave some children open mouthed until they realise that there are many different criteria for making judgements. This links well with building up criteria for looking at works of art, craft and design too.

It is very important to communicate the message – not least in a display – that the process is as important as the end product. When it comes to the point of appraising what has been done, though it may be clear in the teacher's mind, it is anything but clear in many of the children's understanding. It does not necessarily mean that to do something means that you understand what you have done and why you are doing it. We need to communicate to the child what has actually happened, its potential, and what has been achieved. Perhaps none of us realise how many times we expect our children to be thought readers in some contexts! In one sense, the culmination, the finishing of a piece of work and its review, is the greatest step towards the next piece of learning that we have.

The keeping of work is another problem which must be faced in the context of the National Curriculum monitoring and assessment needs. A selection at least of each child's work is necessary for teachers, parents and children to be able to see developmental practice and be able to discuss it. There have also been strong advocates for young children to be able to take things home. This must be seen in the context of children's learning needs; perhaps for every child whose work is made much of and valued at home, there may well be another whose self-image is not helped by the way in which it is received, not taken care of, or even rubbished.

Judicious use of the folder or collection of work can be seen to be one of the best ways to celebrate what has been done, to allow for it to be seen in sequence in retrospect.

Part II

4 Building on experience

This chapter deals with examples of practical work and how it came about. It comes from a large number of children and teachers from different kinds of schools.

The main message it communicates is that vigorous art and design is generated through deliberate structuring and positive means. It never comes from a vacuum, and seldom from throwing children on to their own choices when they do not have the experiential background to deal with it. Where children are able to deal with their own initiatives in all but exceptional cases it is because their lives in school or outside have been rich in enthusiasm, first-hand experience, lively conversation and word usage, good tools and materials, and encouragement to act confidently on their own. The teaching in fact has taken place throughout the child's time in school and elsewhere, and includes the environment and ethos, offering a secure place from which to practise independence.

In art and design education nothing need be out of the context of the whole experiential content of the curriculum, and one thing can be seen to lead quite naturally to another. Teachers who from the beginning of a child's time in school are used to thinking and saying, 'Where can we go from here? What might we do next or develop further?' soon gain confidence in the fact that many children have ideas and will naturally want to make a sequence of pieces of work when the 'one turn, or one piece of work only' expectation is removed. It may be necessary if work is organised on a basis of 'turns', to have longer gaps between working practices, but the obvious development which is so often evident usually outweighs any problems caused. The teacher's evaluation leads to an understanding of the direction the work is taking and an awareness of the need to strengthen certain aspects of approach and practice building on the energy engendered by a good project. Visual and tactile experience from first-hand resources can be continually built up throughout in the form of perceptual work in two and three dimensions, and can become an ever growing bank of resources to generate and inform later work. This can take place in school and elsewhere and can engage teachers in strategies for home work to be understood as a part of the continuum rather than a series of unrelated items or subjects which have little to do with research, personal communication and expression.

Dancing. Special school

AMBER, 4 years

Cat at the Vet *was drawn from a real experience. Oliver the cat had to go to the vet for an injection and Amber went too. It was all very dramatic because the vet bent the needle and the event impressed her. The drawing expresses the whole scenario very well. The vet is looming over the cat brandishing the syringe and there is real eye contact between the determined vet and the anxious cat.*

'We were sorting out the paintbox so everything – the rollers, the brushes and paints were all out. Amber's one year old sister wanted to paint too which created a nice busy atmosphere. At first Amber was playing with the paint and other materials. She wanted to try out everything as she hadn't painted for a while. In the fourth painting of her pet rabbits she was really concentrating. She has two rabbits and she had done drawings of them before but not a painting. She was quite tired after this painting and decided that this was the end of the session.'

ELEANOR, 4½ years

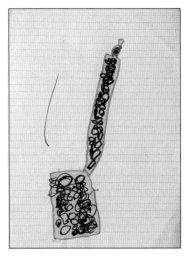

'Giraffe'. Felt tip pen

'Me sitting on a chair with a cat on the floor'

'Lion'

'A big giant with a cat'

As soon as she woke Eleanor was adamant that she wanted to paint because she needed to paint her 'night picture'. Using ready mixed paint she began on the left-hand side with the abstract image to describe her dream and then she painted herself asleep alongside holding her bedtime toy. When she had finished she pointed at the images in turn and said 'This is my dream and this is me holding my favourite rabbit'.

This picture followed immediately and she talked about it as she worked. 'This is your home which I am painting with me inside wearing some dressing-up clothes.' To describe the inside window frames without any prompting she used the end of her brush and drew into the wet paint.

ALICE
5 years

All the pieces of work included here were carried out by Alice who is five years old. She is in Year 1 class in school. She has plenty of opportunity to draw and paint in school and at home. Her class teacher believes that young children should have a wide experience of work based on observation and she is also interested in introducing them to works of art and giving them opportunities to respond, discuss their findings, and base work on what they feel about them. She organises a trip with Years 1 and 2 to the Tate Gallery annually (this is not a London school) and says that the children have been brilliant in response to the experience. Artists' work studied in Year 1 include Wassily Kandinsky, Jackson Pollock, the Pre-Raphaelites, the Impressionists and Mark Rothko. They have worked on a topic on colour and light.

Alice has two older sisters who both enjoy art and often work at home. As soon as Alice began to paint and draw she was dissatisfied by anything other than the tools and materials she saw her sisters using, and she handles them very well. She has a highly characteristic way of working, when faced with a new material or set of tools, of exploring what they will do rather than diving into a painting or drawing. A good example of this is 'Exploration (p74) when she was presented with a new watercolour box of good quality colours and brushes.

She loves colour and responded with great pleasure to paintings by Michael Chase when her family visited his house and studio. She became very excited and enthusiastic and wanted to paint a picture when she got home. An example of her work following this visit is shown (p 74, middle right).

MM talked to Alice about her painting.

MM   *Do you like Michael Chase's paintings?*
ALICE   Yes
MM   *Why do you like them?*
ALICE   Because they are nice
MM   *What is nice about them?*
ALICE   They are bright sort of colours.
MM   *What kind of colours are they?*
ALICE   Sort of mixed up colours. They are red, pink, green, black, blue, brown – I don't know – oh yellow sort of orangy colours and I could see white in places.
MM   *What kind of shapes are in the paintings?*
ALICE   Sort of lines, triangles – there's a tree that is sort of round.
MM   *What were you doing when you did your painting?*
ALICE   My painting has lots of greens and mixed up colours and some red. I like doing lots of shapes and lines and dotty patterns and lots and lots of colours. It's just all about shapes.

The class watched a video on Monet and looked at some reproductions of his work. They were told a story called 'Linnea' which further developed the subject. A class discussion then took place about Monet's paintings. The children were then asked to write their own passage about Monet and his work. Alice wrote:

Monet was an artist. He would paint paintings again and again. He would paint outdoors. He made a bridge. He liked to paint lovely pictures. He made a painting of some ladies in the garden. He liked to paint his garden. If you get very close [to his paintings] it looks all splodgy but if you get far away it looks real. He didn't like to paint dark colours. When he got older he couldn't see.

Her father, who is interested in computers, brought home a new colour printer. Her mother told us that Alice immediately said she would like to do a picture and that she would do one like Monet as she had been talking about him and looking at his work that day. 'After a bit of experimentation, as she was using an art programme she had not used before, she started to work very intently. I came in to see her and she told me that she was doing 'the river picture'. As this was a picture that I was unfamiliar with I found a copy of it in a book and we had a good look and a talk about it while Alice was working on it. She looked very intently at the colours, especially of the sun's reflection in the river, naming the colours and trying to reproduce this effect on the computer. She enjoyed the huge range of colours available to her and the way that she could adjust the thickness of the paint brush. She chose to have a canvas effect. In all the picture would have taken her over an hour. She was slightly disappointed with the printout as the results were much duller than on the screen.' Later Alice said:

> It's a picture with two people in a boat and a setting sun, and you can see the reflection in the water and there's two pine trees and you can see they are reflecting in the water. I did my own picture of the picture. I made it up, but I did look at the picture – it's Monet's picture. (p 74 bottom right)

'Two people and two cats' (p 74 bottom left)

'It's you and me standing in your garden and there's Cassy and Corrie (cats) in there too, and we are walking and there is flowers. There's blue in between the sun's little gaps. The sky's all blue with a little bit of brown in it. The blue goes around the sun and around the other parts.

There's blue, red, pink, reddy brown, red, then pink, red purple and not purple, and Corrie is walking towards me. One (figure)'s bigger and one's smaller and that's you and me and they've got blue eyes and smiley faces and little noses, and Cassy's walking in the plants.'

Pen explorations. Blue ink. 21 x 30 cms

Exploration. Water colour. 8 x 29 cms

Alice at work

Michael Chase 'Abruzzi before dusk', water colour

Alice's water colour after a visit to Michael Chase's studio. 19 x 15cms

'Two people and two cats'. Water colour. 21 x 15 cms

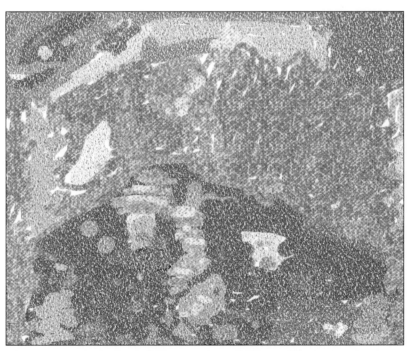

Alice's computer image after seeing Monet's impression. 14 x 18 cms

INFANT PAINTINGS

There will always be a place for paintings, drawings and
models to appear unheralded as part of the working day,
and often based on events, thoughts and memories.
These are some examples.

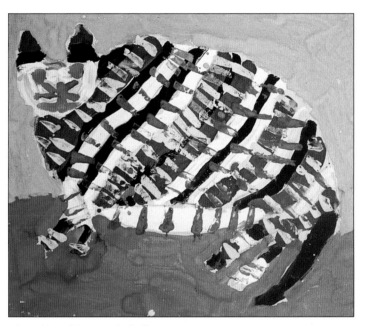

Cat. 42 x 47 cms. Girl, 6 years

Skipping. Girl, 5 years. 58 x 40 cms.

A friend's farm. Girl 5 years. 31 x 51 cms.
*'With a dog, sheep and some cockerels. Cars are going by in the road, the sun is going
down and the moon is coming up'.*

RECEPTION CLASS, INNER CITY SCHOOL
4–5 years

In this school, the early years policy stresses the needs of the 'whole child' and the central place of play – exploration and experimentation - across the curriculum. It is also considered important to praise children for perseverence, and their ability to work through difficulties and show resilience when things appear to go wrong.

As many children start school with a very product-oriented attitude, teachers make a point of only sending pieces of work home every few weeks, the main body of drawings and paintings being kept at school in folders and sketchbooks. When a child does a particularly good piece of work, teachers draw parents' attention to it in their books or on display. This also enables teachers, parents and children to see progress. It allows teachers to reinforce the vocabulary of art, for example 'Look how much detail you put in your drawing now' or 'See how closely you have looked at the texture in the last drawing'.

There is a high profile display in the classroom as this is considered to be part and parcel of the teaching. There are many possible themes which may be used, or qualities and elements. For example, hard/soft, rough/smooth, shape/texture, colour/pattern. After a while the children begin to bring in their own items which are shown, talked about, looked at – sometimes with magnifying glasses - and put on display. Many children become adept at seeing the interest in a bit of stone, a twig or a seed for example. In the last two weeks children have presented teachers with a sheep's backbone, an enormous bracket fungus, a dead wasp, and a very large spider from 'under the bed'. The latter has been kept in a plastic container for closer study. This spider went home in the holiday to be looked after – with some trepidation on the part of the parent.

The children handle, look at, study and talk about the displays constantly. There are often stick insects, frogs, ladybirds and woodlice being cared for for short periods and many more things of interest and learning potential. Any of these experiences may be incorporated into their writing or art, and are linked with books in the class. There is a good supply of books including many covering art and relevant information. The children often choose these for quiet reading times.

Although the children have access to painting and drawing every day, specific art teaching sessions are built into the curriculum. These are in groups of not more than six children so that a lot of individual attention can be offered.

In regard to observational drawing the teacher said, 'If we challenged them to look at our tortoise shell, for example, we would spend a lot of time handling it and finding out as much about it as we could. We would also think what it reminds us of, and what it could be used for. In my class some of the suggestions were a fruit bowl, a helmet, a water carrier, and a potty if you were stuck in a traffic jam and couldn't get to a toilet (obviously based on memory and a felt need!). One child suggested setting it into a ring for a giant.' The feeling is that all activities are about opening up possibilities in the children's thinking and looking.

An important point stressed throughout in regard to what happens in the class is the matter of mutual trust. 'It takes time,' said the class teacher, 'to develop confidence for many children and it can only happen where they feel totally accepted. When the trust does develop then children can be freed from anxiety about making mistakes. It also means that you can have high expectations of the effort they put in, which so often seems to lead to better quality work. When children rush something, or don't put their heart into it, it seems more respectful to them to say so. I would say something like, 'I can see you're not as interested in doing this as usual, do you want to leave it now and come back to it later?'

Perhaps the most important but difficult thing to assess is the ambience within a class. As a teacher my classroom has to interest me as well as the children. When I come in the morning I want to feel excited – especially on those days when I am tired or fed up. When the classroom offers a lot visually, it can be a source of ideas that can feed into your planning, or see you through a low patch.

The children pick up on the teacher attitude inevitably. When they sense a real interest in them and what they do and say, they blossom. By the end of their reception year I hope that no child will come to me and say 'I don't know what to do'. Through our teaching they are helped to make choices and work independently as much as possible.'

This school has made a particular effort to come to terms with the need to enable staff and children to have resource stimuli to hand. A sum of money was set aside to build up collections of stimuli, and a room was set aside for housing this 'museum'.

LISA: some work during one year

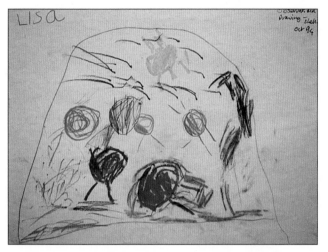

September. Observational drawing: tortoise shell

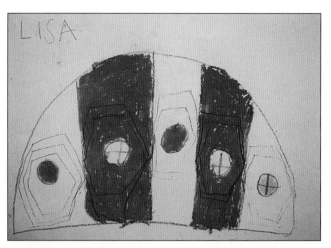

January. Observational drawing: tortoise shell

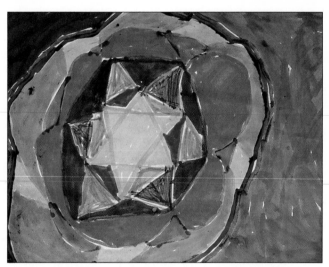

March. Pattern

April. Observational drawing: tortoise shell

April. Drawing based on pond weed

May. 'The tunnel'. Imaginative work based in a story. A black circle was stuck onto the paper by the teacher as a starting point

May. Pattern

May. Self portrait

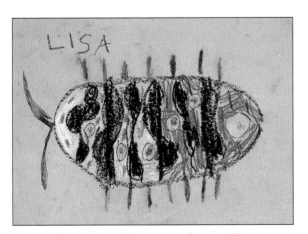

May. Observational drawing of a woodlouse

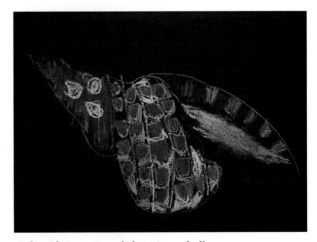

July. Observational drawing: shell

It is interesting to note Lisa's development over this year. She has been encouraged, and has chosen to return to particular challenges, and each time she does shows more understanding, and greater control of media. A number of other particular challenges are apparent, and it is important to remember that it is through these also that the development is built up

MOTHER AND CHILD PROJECTS 1, 2 & 3

Project 1: 5 and 6 year old class

'This was linked to a topic on 'Ourselves'. Every child brought in two photographs, one of themselves as a baby and one as a three year old. One of the parents brought in her newborn baby to show us. She fed, cleaned and changed her, and the children asked questions. The next step was an experimental session where charcoal, soft pencils, felt tipped pens, oil and chalk pastels and graphite sticks were introduced. I had photocopies of black and white newspaper eyes and cut them out. Each child had one to stick on to their paper before trying out all the materials in any way they wished. I have found that any stimulus such as a shape or mark seems to liberate the children as it seems to give them a way into their work. Some of them spent up to an hour on this drawing. I tried to encourage the children who said they had 'finished' by saying things like, 'The marks you have made with the oil pastel look really creamy, have you seen what the charcoal can do?' They took a lot of inspiration from other children's ways of working.

After our experimentation we put them up in the corridor and discussed them. The variation in approach, and sense of composition in some of them was very interesting.

We then looked at mother and child paintings and sculptures from India, and some done by Henry Moore.

The next step was to draw from a model, children taking it in turns to sit holding a large baby doll. They were encouraged in this drawing to use whatever materials and tools they liked. The 'model' wore a black-and-white checked dress as I wanted to see what they made of this problem.

As they worked I tried to draw their attention to the sitter and the doll. I asked questions – 'Can you see the legs?' 'Where is the baby?' and so on. Some children finished in fifteen minutes, but many worked for a full hour and a quarter session. A few wanted to break off, but came back later. Seeing how good some of the drawings were inspired many children to go on with their own pictures.

When they were all completed we used them as a basis for our assembly, and later displayed them in the school hall.'

Class teacher

Exploration of tools and materials

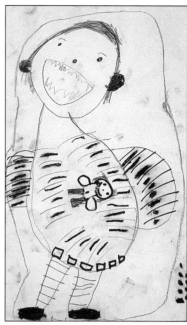

Reception children, 5 years. 30 x 25 cms

PROJECT 2: 8 years

'The children worked in clay on the theme and looked at all kinds of mother and child imagery as well as family photographs. These drawings in oil pastel were the results of developing ideas.'

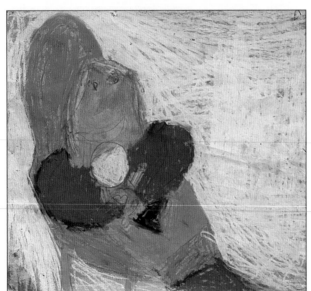

Work from a mother and child project, 8 years

PROJECT 3: 9 and 10 year old class

'It was decided that the whole year's main art focus for our 9 and 10 year olds would be on the human body, in order to develop observation skills and drawing.

In the autumn term within the theme of the Ancient Egyptians the children looked at figures on tomb wall paintings and noticed that though the faces and legs were in profile, the bodies were frontal. Following sketchbook experiment, they drew profiles of each other in a seated position. The spring term topic on 'Living Things' included thinking about the human body and how it worked. The final term's theme of 'The Victorians' returned us to portraits, but this time full-length figures and family groups. The year's work culminated with real models (a parent and daughter) being invited to sit for the whole class to draw.

Throughout the whole project the children were shown the work of artists and invited to discuss it. They chose their own materials and were given opportunities to experiment. As the children worked I tried asking questions to help them think more carefully. For example, 'How does the little girl's dress look from here? Is it spread or straight?' 'Where are her Mum's knees?' 'Can you see all of her face?' 'Are her feet bigger than her Mum's?'

82

Finally I point out what has been done well, or what is interesting, to celebrate the different approaches and styles so that the children develop a wider appreciation themselves of what goes to make an interesting, exciting or unusual piece of art.

Children need time to change their minds, and chances to try several times, so that they are happy with what they achieve.'

Class teacher

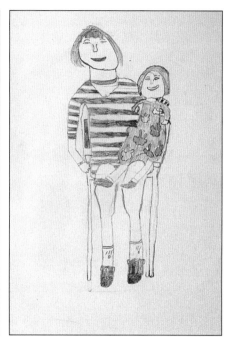

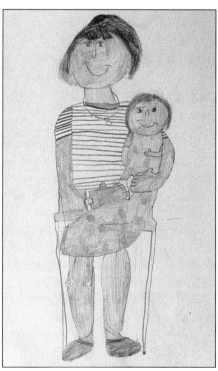

Work from a mother and child project, 9 and 10 years

THE ROSENDALE ODYSSEY
A cross-curricular media-arts project for 4-7 year olds

Arib photographing Daniel

Jessica talking about her family album pictures

Rosendale Infants School in South London has 320 children from a culturally diverse community. 22 different languages are spoken by pupils (and staff) of African, Caribbean, Asian, Latin American, Chinese and European descent.

Background: The Rosendale Odyssey media-arts project was initiated as a collaboration between Rosendale Infants and the Photographers' Gallery, with artists Dave Lewis, Shona Illingworth and Julie Myers working in residence for one school year. Rather than taking a nostalgic look at Victorian schooldays, the school's approaching centenary was seen as an opportunity for the children to creatively investigate their own families, histories and experiences, exploring changes and celebrating diversity. Cross-curricular, it involved the whole school in a multimedia storytelling project, using photography, video, drawing, digital imaging, sound and text. The software programme *Hyperstudio* brought together all these media, the resulting multimedia 'stacks' now forming the basis of an online project designed by Julie. The children built up a picture of their personal histories to share and explore with one another and the school now has a valuable media-arts resource to develop new work from. The Website (http://www.artec.org.uk/rosendale) will create a global audience, inviting participation from other schools, locally and internationally.

Themes and tools: The broad themes – introduced by slides shown to each year group just before the artists' work commenced – were as follows: history, geography, communication, family, identity, memory and photography. Photography was a tool as well as a theme since developmental work in the first term involved examining photographs, questioning how we encounter and use them, exploring composition, framing etc. With the approaching centenary, history was an underlying thread. English skills played an integral part, as did various issues from PSHE.

Besides traditional art and design materials, tools included basic 'point and shoot' cameras, the children's photographs, an audio-cassette recorder, a digital camera, a scanner and three Apple Macintosh Power PC Computers.

The Rosendale Odyssey was an ambitious, multi-stranded project. The Photographers' Gallery has a history of school-based education work, but this was its largest initiative ever: given the main aims and themes, it was essential to work over a year, right across the school[1]. For the work to act as a model of practice, therefore, we tried to devise something that would divide into smaller, easily adaptable themes, not necessarily dependent on 'cutting edge' technology. Indeed, much of the follow-up work undertaken by teachers in class was done with basic primary materials. Smaller themes included: family albums, memories, journeys, postcards, family trees, names, appearance, hairstyles, food and recipes, locality, school, home.

Memory, for example, was examined and developed as follows. First the artists recounted their earliest memories to the class. The children were then invited to do the same, some being very keen, others shy – so a corner of the library was used as a 'videobox', where one child sat on the 'memory blanket' recalling stories to the video camera operated by another. An early drawing session also made 'First Memories' its theme. Letters were sent home requesting old family photographs. These were compared with pictures pupils had taken of each other and became the basis for extensive painting, drawing, writing and multimedia activities. To explore the differences between the photographic recording of events and our memories, children were asked to extend the frame, drawing what the camera had left out. Parents and carers were encouraged to participate by providing artefacts and information from family archives and by answering questionnaires devised in class about their memories.

1 In additional to the school and gallery, this project was funded by The Sir John Cass Foundation, Gulbenkian Foundation, The Walcott Educational Foundation and sponsored by Kodak. It was also supported by ARTEC (Arts Technology Centre, London) and Middlesex University and the research was funded by The Arts Council of England.

Shona Illingworth showing digital camera pictures to a Year 2 class

All these initial sessions were carried out with a whole class, children from one class explaining what they had done to the next class to do the activity. 'Showback' and questions were encouraged at the end of each session. Two photographic artists worked with Year 1 (Dave) and Year 2 (Shona), while Fiona Bailey, the gallery's project officer, worked with Reception and Nursery. In this developmental phase children explored new tools and key themes, leading on to computer work in the second and third terms.

Artists working in school can be stimulating for children and teachers. It can also be problematic. School culture is very specific and there has to be negotiation and clear communication between artists and teachers before and during the project. Planning and discussion were vital to ensure that expectations matched and project work could be prioritised on days when artists were working, or else developed by teachers outside this time. This did not always happen, but was improved over time and constantly reviewed to assess effectiveness.

An integrated formative research and evaluation strategy was implemented from the outset, extending beyond the residency and production period into Phase 2, to end the following school year. We could thus examine several important educational issues, including:

- To what extent might use of (various) media technologies help young people create and control a self image?

- How might working with media artists enhance and extend the children's creative opportunities and communicative abilities?

Seeing themselves in photographs, on video and computer certainly made the children more aware of how they looked but it also made them more aware of each other. Interest in one another's work increased markedly, especially when the *Hyperstudio* pieces were shown back in class. Shy pupils and children with difficulties seemed particularly to benefit – the work increased their confidence by validating everyone's experiences.

Working with the artists definitely extended possibilities, giving many children access to new technologies as creative tools: especially positive was the effect of visual work on their speaking, listening and creative writing skills. With three computers shared between so many, equal access was always an issue. Most had hands-on experience but those who got less will require further opportunities in Phase 2.

Further developments: For new children we hope the work will be a resource; for those who worked on it, a basis for developing further ideas and technical skills. The nature of Internet culture being one of transformation, the school website will now be the main area for developing work, as a point of exchange between many different schools.

Training has been a central element of this project. All the teachers have had a basic introduction to the software and hardware used, and to the Internet's potential. In Phase 2, training will be more advanced, aimed at the school's IT co-ordinator and project manager, to ensure expertise remains within the school and to allow the website to develop, so that both the technology and the project-as-resource continue to be used to full their potential.

Rebecca Sinker is currently a Research Fellow in Photography & Media Education, based at Middlesex University, working in partnership with The Photographers' Gallery and ARTEC. She is responsible for the documentation and evaluation of the Rosendale Odyssey.

Roisin's bedroom

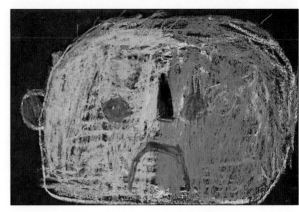

Joseph's memory of tests at the hospital

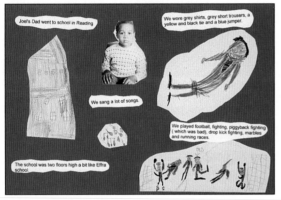

Joel's father's memories of school

Louis' book about himself

Julian as a baby with his grandma

Carmen (extending the frame)

Rebecca (extending the frame)

Lucy (extending the frame)

Damien, Reception

This is a picture of my Mum and my Grandma. I think this picture is very old . I think my mum looks like she is six. I think this picture was taken in Jamaica. My Grandma doesn't look like this anymore because she is a grandma now.

my grandmas wedding

Halima, Reception

This is me on a bus going past my house. I live in London. Before I lived in England I lived in India. I came on an aeroplane. It was the first time on an aeroplane. It was like being in a rocket going through the sky. I like India because all my friends play with me. In India it is warm all day.

Sahil, Reception

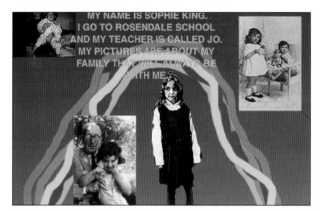

MY NAME IS SOPHIE KING. I GO TO ROSENDALE SCHOOL AND MY TEACHER IS CALLED JO. MY PICTURES ARE ABOUT MY FAMILY THAT WILL ALWAYS BE WITH ME.

Sophie, Year 1

THIS WAS MY HOUSE IN PORTUGAL. IT WAS VERY HOT.

Licinia, Year 1

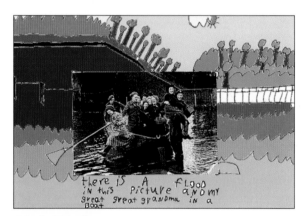

there is A FLOOD in this picture and my great great grandma in a boat

Mark, Year 2

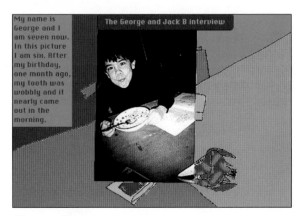

My name is George and I am seven now. In this picture I am six. After my birthday, one month ago, my tooth was wobbly and it nearly came out in the morning.

The George and Jack B interview

George, Year 2

dad in Jamaica

My Mum in Korea

My friends

My dad and mum have different grandmas and grandads. they come from different countries. My mum is called Chung Hay and my dad is called Antonio.

Annabelle, Year 2

OUR WORLD WEEK
Whole School
project 5–11 years

In a world of many cultures, a world seemingly shrinking in size as transport, communications and media bring life across the waters closer to home; as children experience travel abroad whether on holiday or through books and television, it is clear that the influences of the world's cultures are leaving their mark on society.

The objective of 'Our World Week' was to raise the children's awareness of other countries and their cultures, and to celebrate the similarities and the differences.

For one week the thirteen-class primary school went on a world 'journey'. Each day we visited a different part of the globe. Five of the six continents were represented – India, the United Kingdom, Ghana, Australia and Brazil, with special focus on the arts aspect in each culture.

One of the two halls was transformed into a multi-cultural centre with areas filled with costumes, pictures, photographs, posters, materials, artefacts, food, books and music. The classes visited this area daily to work with the displays, to sketch and paint from the artefacts, design costumes and explore cultural uses of pattern, listen to stories and taste the food.

The other hall was devoted to our visiting artists. Traditional Indian dancers, an Aborigine storyteller from Australia, music and drama workshops from Ghana, a Brazilian band showing us the excitement of the carnival, and our own country dance tradition gave stimulus for a variety of work including school performances and class workshops.

In the classrooms the children explored the history and geography of the lands they were 'visiting'. They cooked and ate the food, listened to the stories, sang the songs and experienced many of the skills and styles used in the various countries – from face painting, dot brooches and seed clay patterns in Australia to batik, tie dye and printmaking in India. The use of the artefacts, pictures and costumes inspired high standards of printmaking, tie dye designs, head dresses, masks, three-dimensional work with clay and dough, boomerang and jewellery design, batik, a rainforest collage and painting. The children created an interactive rainforest where a multi-sensory experience could be explored. The ideas from staff and children developed as the week progressed.

After months of preparation we believed we had met our aim; and it was rewarding also to see clearly from the children's work a progression throughout the key stages. There had been an atmosphere of togetherness, not just as a school but with the wider world. Skills and interests were nurtured and developed. Ideas and ideals for the future were firmly planted in us all.

Class teacher

One of the displays in the hall

First day – looking at India

Child in Indian national costume

Interactive rainforest

Children exploring and drawing in the rainforest

Drum from Ghana

Indian weaving figure

Ghanaian workshop activities

Whole school workshop with music and dancing

Children making Australian cave pictures on clay tablets

Indian dance workshop

Designing Ghanaian patterns for tee shirts

Sketching from artefacts in the hall

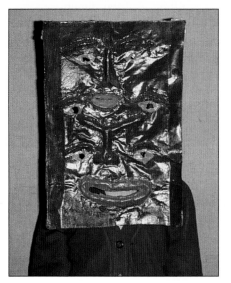
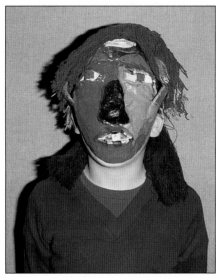

Papier maché masks

Soft sculptured heads

WORKING WITH ETHNIC OBJECTS
9 and 10 years

Introducing artefacts from other cultures is stimulating and challenging. This project concerns the responses of a group of ten year old children to ethnic images and objects, culminating in a visit to the Museum of Mankind in London.

Session 1: Introduction

We discussed the various challenges to be undertaken during the project, and explored available materials and alternative ways of working.

The children tried on some original masks from Papua New Guinea, to get the feel of what they were going to experience later on. They were also introduced to other source material, for example images of ethnic objects on postcards and in books, in preparation for Session 2 when they were going to make a mask. We talked about masks and the idea that they could be something behind which you could hide or assume a new identity. We suggested that they could search for additional images and information themselves.

Session 2: Making the mask

During this session the children were offered a selection of postcards depicting masks, and invited to choose one or more to act as a starting point for making a three-dimensional mask or soft sculptured head. Those deciding to use papier maché needed little advice as most of them were already familiar with the technique and the need to rest the balloon on an open ice-cream tub to keep the working side uppermost. Their enthusiasm for working in three dimensions was soon evident. One mask (p 91, top left) was created by forming a papier maché shell over one balloon and then another placed at right angles. This was the maker's own development after he had worked for some time with a postcard illustration of a wooden Mexican Aztec mask decorated with turquoise mosaic. He decided after a number of attempts that the mosaic was too difficult but he continued to refer to the image while also looking at others. He wrote: 'I found that most masks don't have many teeth and their ears stick out at right angles. I enjoyed making the mask because it was successful but it was hard to make.'

Session 3: Detailed drawing of pattern

The purpose of this session was to study pattern and colour in masks. We had in the classroom a large mask from Papua New Guinea carved from one piece of wood. The design on it was complex and detailed. One child who drew the whole mask in one sitting must have drawn without erasing for about an hour. Others found the whole design too challenging and concentrated on a small area.

Session 4: Working with primitive figures

A small collection of carved primitive figures was brought into the classroom and the children drew from them. Again this was partly in preparation for the visit to the Museum of Mankind. We discussed the way in which aspects of the figure were emphasised, distorted, exaggerated or incised with pattern to convey mood and feeling.

Session 5: Interaction with primitive objects: a day in the Museum of Mankind

This was the highlight of the project. A 'handling session' had been arranged so that the children could encounter and draw from authentic masks and figures. Initially the children spent some time touching the sculptures and trying on masks. They were also told something of their meaning and purpose. They then drew from these artefacts for an hour and a half. In this way they were able to use feeling, memory and visual clues to inform their drawing. The preparation sessions were important but this first-hand experience of the objects was a vital ingredient in the quality of the work achieved.

Class teacher

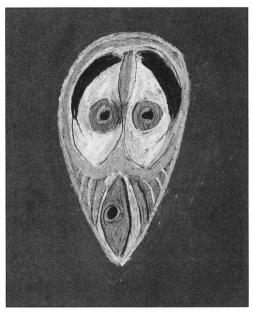

Mask: pastel drawing

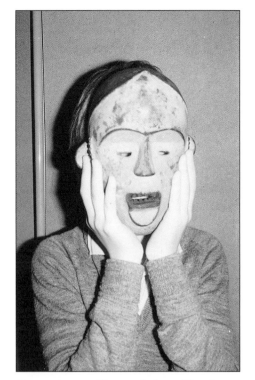

Boy trying on Ibo mask from Nigeria

10 year olds working from artefacts in the Museum of Mankind

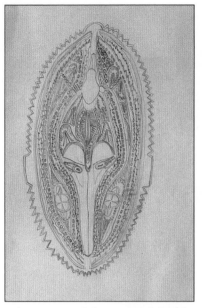

*Observational drawing of shield
from Papua New Guinea. 10 years*

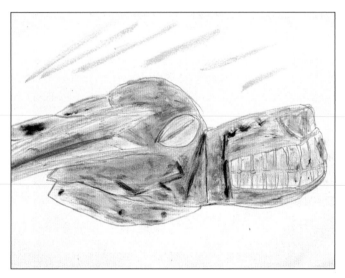

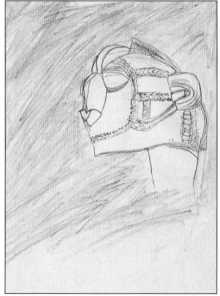

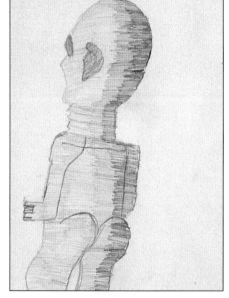

Drawings from artefacts in the Museum of Mankind

QUILTS (p 96)

The Writtle quilt, designed by 7 and 8 year old children from drawings made in the local environment. 2 x 1 m

Quilt designed by 5 year olds based on Thorndon Country Park. 1 x 2 m

An example of the sketches made in the Thorndon park which formed the basis for the children's designs

Detail from Thorndon quilt showing individual work

Examples of the Writtle sketches from which the transfer crayon drawings were made

Detail from Writtle quilt showing individual work

QUILTS

Project 1:
The Thorndon Country Park Quilt
5 years

Our quilt was made as part of a whole school project, which was based on the theme of the natural environment.

In the autumn we had a whole school trip to a local country park. My class enjoyed kicking throught the leaves, climbing over fallen tree trunks and collecting coloured leaves, conkers, chestnuts, stones, twigs, seedheads and acorns. Later we looked at the items we had collected and the photographs of the trip, pictures of the autumn, the fruits of the trees and bushes, the colours of the leaves, patterns in seedheads, the light through branches and how it dapples the leaves on the ground. The children decided what they wanted to record and the quilt became a patchwork of each child's memories of that day.

To begin with the children each had a sheet of paper onto which they drew their design. These sketches were then kept in a large book, so that the children had easy access to them and could refer back when they came to use the fabrics. They were given a piece of white cotton material, and we discussed how they could recreate their picture on the material. The decision was made to use mainly felt for our quilt because felt does not fray, it is easy for small hands to cut if they are given sharp scissors which they have been taught to use, and it can be glued in place as well as being sewn. However they were involved in experimenting with different kinds of stitches. The children had access to a selection of made up brusho mixtures, so that they could colour their background if they wished. It was interesting to note the children's responses to their original design as some adhered exactly to the original design, some altered or embellished it and some changed their minds completely. Some of them cut out their drawings and pinned them on to the felt to cut round, while others used them as templates and drew round them.

The quilt now hangs in the hall. The last word goes to the child who sat and looked at the quilt on the wall and said wistfully, 'And even when I've gone to the juniors, this will still be here!'

Class teacher

Project 2:
The Writtle Quilt
7 and 8 years

Like many successful projects The Writtle Quilt evolved rather than being the result of detailed planning from the beginning; though each stage was carefully managed to ensure that the children gained from the experience.

The children were studying their local environment, and visits to the village green provided an excellent opportunity to carry out some sketching. The class teacher, together with a parent, an artist and the teacher assistant, took the children to the green and encouraged them to complete two or three pencil sketches of the buildings, plants and wild life they observed.

Delighted with their pictures, the children clearly wanted to use their sketches as a basis for further art work, and the adults suggested they design the squares of a quilt. The children chose their favourite sketches and drew them in detail within a 15cm square. The pictures were coloured with fabric crayon, ironed on to polycotton and hand quilted. The children worked in small groups with support and once the individual squares were completed they became involved in the exercise of joining them together. The children then backed the quilt with fabric.

The children were involved in a variety of curriculum areas: *Art* – sketching, creating a design from a sketch, use of pencils and fabric crayons, use of a variety of textile skills including transfer printing, stitching and quilting; *Maths* – tessellation of shapes, area, multiplication, mirror images; *Science* – observation skills, knowledge of wildlife; *History* – observation of historic buildings; *Language* – discussion; *Personal and social skills* – working as a team, involvement in a long-term project.

The finished hanging has been much admired. The class are delighted with their quilt, not only because the result is very pleasing but also because they have been totally involved in all aspects of its production.

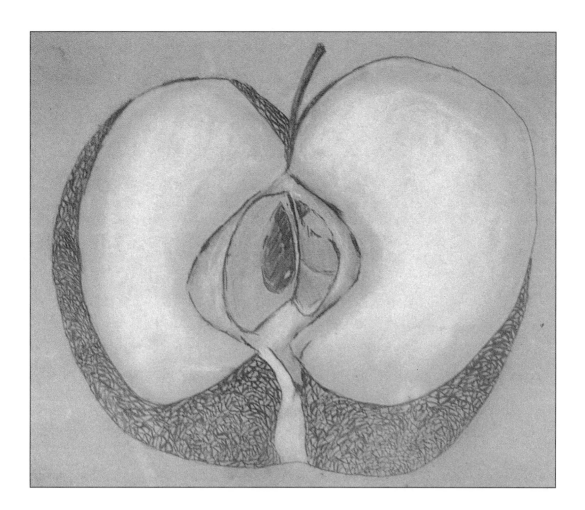

THE APPLE PROJECT
No. 1: 9 year olds
(Cockayne's Orchard)

At the beginning of the autumn term it was arranged for the class to visit Cockayne's Orchard, an apple farm near the school. Members of staff thought it would be a wonderful experience for the children to be in a fruiting orchard at this time of the year, and a number of parents worked there. It also offered good potential for useful cross-curricular experience.

The children were prepared in school before the visit. Autumn was discussed, and the year and life cycle of fruit trees. Ways of harvesting and processing fruit were considered, and general points in regard to food values. Other apple growing areas of the world were introduced, but the most important thing was to be the visit itself. Not only would the children be challenged to look at how the fruit was grown and processed, they would be encouraged to enjoy the experience of being there, and being aware of the atmosphere, and sensory learning. Colour, shape, pattern, texture and form experience should be taken into account.

The actual visit included guided tours organised for groups of children by the owner, the foreman and other people who worked there. Much time was spent in the orchard looking at trees and fruit and watching the pickers at work. Other parts of the tour included being taken to see the apples being sorted and packed, and to study the machinery used and the refrigerators for storage. At the end of a happy day the children returned to school with a lot of new knowledge and experience, and a large box of apples.

Follow up work in the school was based on the flow chart diagram on page 100, and cross-curricular work was successfully begun.

The following spring the children looked at the apple trees and blossom, and made observational drawings and paintings.

97

*Paintings
and drawings
from folk stories*

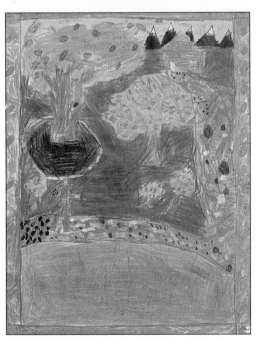

*The Apple Orchard. Paint, graphic
media, group collage*

98

Apple batik. Group work

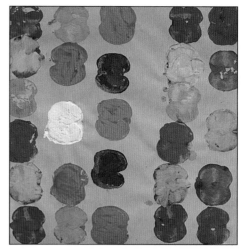

Apple prints. Colour focus

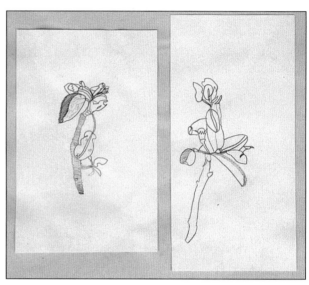

Observational drawings

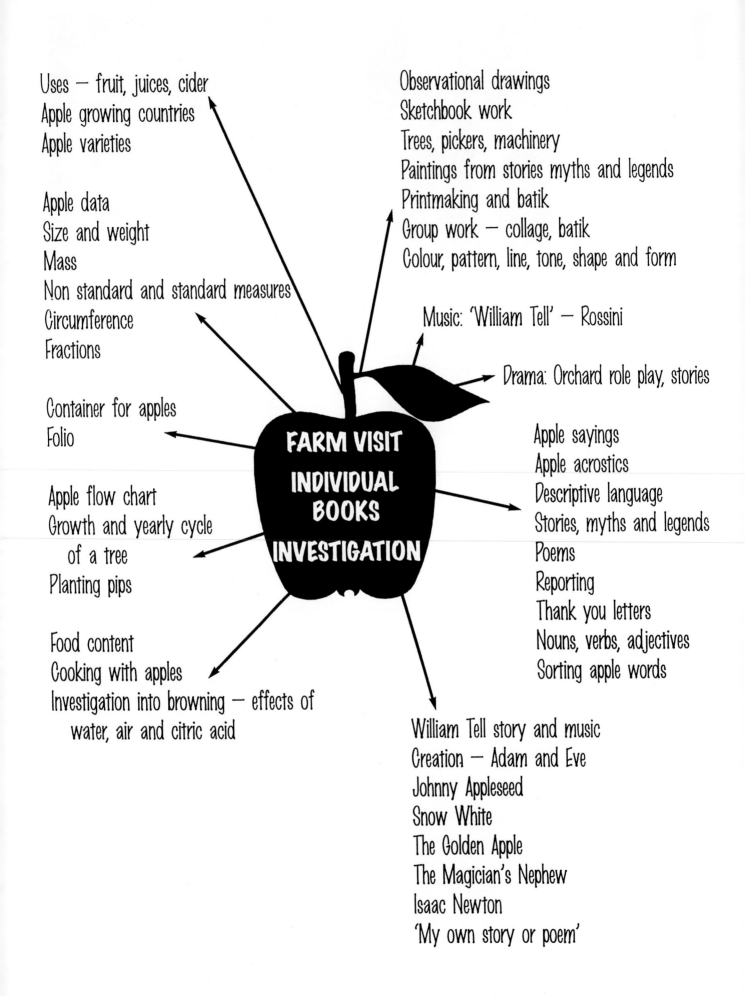

Uses — fruit, juices, cider
Apple growing countries
Apple varieties

Apple data
Size and weight
Mass
Non standard and standard measures
Circumference
Fractions

Container for apples
Folio

Apple flow chart
Growth and yearly cycle
    of a tree
Planting pips

Food content
Cooking with apples
Investigation into browning — effects of
    water, air and citric acid

Observational drawings
Sketchbook work
Trees, pickers, machinery
Paintings from stories myths and legends
Printmaking and batik
Group work — collage, batik
Colour, pattern, line, tone, shape and form

Music: 'William Tell' — Rossini

Drama: Orchard role play, stories

Apple sayings
Apple acrostics
Descriptive language
Stories, myths and legends
Poems
Reporting
Thank you letters
Nouns, verbs, adjectives
Sorting apple words

FARM VISIT

**INDIVIDUAL
BOOKS**

INVESTIGATION

William Tell story and music
Creation — Adam and Eve
Johnny Appleseed
Snow White
The Golden Apple
The Magician's Nephew
Isaac Newton
'My own story or poem'

No. 2:
12 year olds

In the autumn the class discussed orchards and apples which, being in a rural area, they would all be familiar with. The whole experience was focused by the use of excerpts from Robert Frost's poem 'Apple Picking'. The teacher and children took it in turns to pose on a step ladder brought into the classroom. A number of different poses were taken, and the children worked in their sketchbooks. A selection of the sketches were put to good use as individual paintings were planned and undertaken. The following spring the children looked at apple trees again and made observational studies.

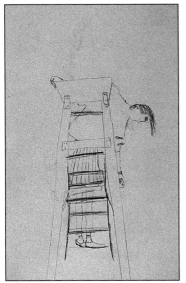

Sketchbook work

Observational drawings

Sketchbook work

Apple picking painting

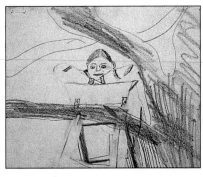

Sketchbook work

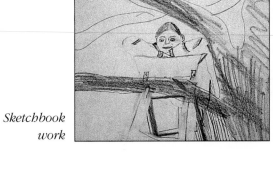

Apple picking painting

Sketchbook work

Apple picking painting

CLAIRE
10 years

Claire is ten years old. She spends a large amount of time in a wheelchair but is able to be out of it for short periods of time. She has cerebral palsy. She has always been in a mainstream school and takes a full part in its life. Claire enjoys art of all kinds and is especially fond of drawing, working sometimes for hours at home and with great concentration.

The drawings shown here are self-explanatory – a day in her life: a challenge for the class suggested by the teacher.

In the pictures on p 104 Claire shows her own pleasure and responses to particular situations – being taken on a roundabout, and on a swing. She has a keen eye and also enjoys depicting what is going on around her and in her imagination. Whatever she draws is marked by intense interest and personal involvement.

MONSTERS AND DRAGONS

Project 1: 5 years

'Monsters' started as a half-term topic, but quickly grew in all directions to encompass dragons, prehistoric monsters and anything else that the children could devise. We read 'The Monster Bed' and played in the 'Cobbaldy Cave' in the role play area. We measured the length of a very friendly soft dragon and wrote monster stories. We were monsters in drama and dance and we read about St George and the Dragon on St George's Day. We met Max and the Wild Things (Maurice Sendak).

Before painting a monster, the children worked out in their sketchbooks ideas of what a monster is like. The resulting paintings were interesting, since some bore a close resemblance to the original ideas and some were completely different, influenced by further stories and books that we had read. One group worked with clay. They explored clay and the properties of the material, squeezing it, pinching it and making holes and 'tunnels', rolling 'worms' and 'sausages'. Then we discussed how we would make our monsters – in one piece, a head only – or how to pull pieces out or join them on to the body using a brush and 'slip' (clay and water mixture). These models were later painted in bright colours.

What did we gain from 'Monsters'? Working with ideas and materials, and new techniques and processes were developed. As well as this we had a lot of fun.

Project 2: 11 years

Concepts
Using examples of Dragons and Beasts from different art periods, pupils will use clay and print to create their own framed representation.

Skills
Use of observational and recording skills, selection, design, clay rolling, slab building and modelling techniques. Decoration and use of colour. Print and rubbings. IT use of scanner.

Teaching methods
Whole class and group work. Discussion and demonstrations and individual attention.

Differentiation
By outcome.

Assessment focus
b Gather resource information and use it to stimulate and develop ideas.
c Explore and use 2 and 3 dimensional media.
d Review and modify their work as it progresses.
e Develop an understanding of the work of artists and apply knowledge to own work.
f Respond to and evaluate own and other's artwork.

Resources
Dragon/Beast resource pack, paper and recording media, clay, paint, card, string, glue, wax crayons, printing materials.

Use of the computer and scanner.

Progression
1 Introduction. Show illustrations from resource pack. Discuss.
2 Record Dragon/Beast information from the resource pack.
3 Decide upon a picture frame shape – cut template
4 Design a dragon to apply as relief decoration to the picture frame – twisting, curling, entwining.
5 Make a small experimental clay test piece, modelling features and scale textures, etc.
6 Make picture frame using clay.

7 Experiment with colour on test piece using paint, etc.

8 Use of print and rubbings/both card and string relief/monoprints using previous design information.

9 Use of scanner and computer to record, compare and combine dragon/beast images.

Homework

1 Design an illuminated letter in a given shape and include a dragon.

2 Design a dragon type repeating pattern that could be used as a decorative border for your picture frames.

3 Title page for your dragons project.

4 Produce a card/string relief printing block.

5 Explain, comic strip style, using a combination of pictures and words, how you made your clay picture frame.

6 Evaluation.

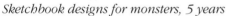

Sketchbook designs for monsters, 5 years

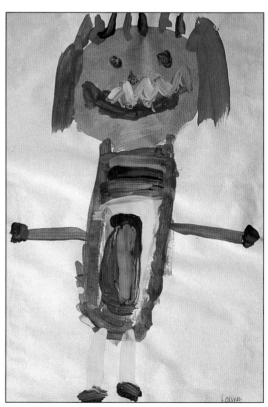

Sketchbook design and development into a painting.
60 x 30 cm

Monster paintings. 30 x 30 cm, 30 x 60 cm

Animal monster. 5 years

5 year olds experimenting and working collaboratively, sticking materials together to make monster models

Human monster 'full of dinner that the monster has eaten'

11–12 year olds. This dragon project was developed using a 'resource stimuli pack' built up by the teachers. Exploration of materials played a major role in developing work

A MIDSUMMER NIGHT'S DREAM
Village primary school

'The idea of introducing Shakespeare to primary age children has become popular recently, particularly with the introduction of the National Curriculum. No doubt with this in mind and the need for a Christmas production for the village the staff at our small primary school decided to tackle a Shakespeare play. It was to be just 45 minutes long, using all our nine and ten year old children (twenty in all) for the major parts and the rest of our Key Stage 2 children in smaller roles. The production had to be relevant, worthwhile and enjoyable and was to be part of our English and Arts programmes.

Clearly if we were going to make this a worthwhile experience for the children we had to do more than just give out the lines and act them out. We decided that the children would be involved in the whole production, including costume design and manufacture, and that this would form a half term in our art programme.

We decided upon *A Midsummer Night's Dream* which had the advantage of being, on the surface, a fairy tale with clear characters, a strong atmosphere and an immediate appeal to children. The script was re-written and shortened with an attempt to make it clear and accessible whilst keeping the general style of language and some of the more famous lines. I am indepted to Leon Garfield's wonderful book *Shakespeare's Tales* which paints the stories beautifully.

The children were also familiar with Elizabethan dialogue, having previously studied the Tudors, and they accepted the script with ease.

Preparations began with the telling of the story and some initial script readings. We talked through the plot and looked at the characters. The children then had to consider the characters in the wood and decide what sort of costumes they would need, based on what they knew of the story.

This was important: a way into the script. For by following this line we were requiring the children to look very closely at the text and analyse what they had read. How could a reasoned judgement be made on a character if the character was not known?

We decided to look at three main areas: texture, colour, shape and line. Each of these areas could be used to suggest the character of the player. Oberon for instance was finally dressed in long heavy dark materials to emphasise his power and the heavy scents of a midsummer night, whilst Cobweb (a fairy) was dressed in light nets, bright and shimmering to reflect not only her character but also her name.

The children's first ideas were quickly sketched - the first draft no more than brief notes or brainstorms and here I purposely liken the task to that of creative writing. The process is the same in both.

For the design sketches we used pen and ink for line and ink wash and wax to add colour, using Arthur Rackham's illustrations and modern fashion designs as a starting point. While working, the children were encouraged to add notes to their drawings. The children were able to check their ideas by examining the textures of different materials or by referring to books and catalogues. These showed how artists had used colour to create atmosphere. Landscapes by Cézanne, Sutherland, and Turner emphasised the point well.

These finished designs were used to produce the final costumes and the production went ahead very successfully. The children had been able to get inside the characters through their art. This gave the play more meaning which in return brought yet more understanding to the children and, it has to be said, the audience as well.'

Headmaster

Design for Puck and Arthur Rackham drawings

Design for Oberon

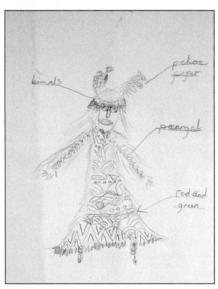

Design for Titania

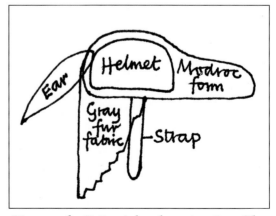

Design for Puck

Design for Bottom

Diagram for Bottom's head construction. 'The head was constructed on an old cycle helmet, built up around crushed paper with Modroc which was lined with material. Ears were made of wire and gauze'.

Oberon

Titania

Puck

Bottom

LONG BRUSH PAINTINGS

Children often find it hard to work in a bold way. In this project hoghair brushes were fixed to bamboo canes, and the children thoroughly enjoyed using them. Paint, water and paper were organised within easy reach on the floor. The subject matter was of other children at work in the room, and they were challenged to paint what they could really see. We asked a pupil to show us how it was done, and he re-enacted the way in which he worked.

Boy, 9 years

Girl, 11 years

Girl, 10 years

Boy, 11 years

Girl, 11 years

THE CASTLE AT MUIDEN
JAN BEERSTRATEN

A village primary school

'The work on Jan Beerstraaten's picture *The Castle at Muiden in Winter* developed from a course run by the National Gallery and attended by one of our staff.

We decided to use the picture throughout the school as a stimulus for art, music, drama and writing, using staff specialisms and those of a postgraduate music student who was spending three weeks with us. The main focus of the work would be that of the strong atmosphere within the painting itself.

The picture was introduced to the whole school (sixty children) and we began by asking them to look very closely at different sections of it which had been previously photocopied. At this point the children were unaware that these pieces were linked. We asked the children to continue the picture using pencil, biro or fibre tip and to try and maintain the same style of working. We asked them to look for clues which might help them in their reconstruction. What was the weather like? What time of year was it? Where was the picture painted – town, country, home, abroad?

Staff then took their classes off to work and we agreed to meet again in the afternoon to look at the drawings and see the original picture.

We asked the children to note down their feelings about the task and how they approached it.

'When I first saw my picture I thought people were old fashioned and were on ice. I thought the other people's pieces might be from the same picture but I wasn't sure. I thought the people were dressed warmly and they were on ice so it made me think it was winter. The end person looked as if he was talking to someone. I couldn't wait to see the rest.' (Girl, 9 years)

'When I first saw the picture I thought, 'Oh no this is going to be hard.' I hadn't a clue what to do but I soon built up my ideas. I thought it was night time in winter. I had an idea to draw the rest of the castle, then the sky and some grass around the castle. I made the grass by doing lots of strokes with my pen and shaded in the trunk of my tree with my pencil. I did light and dark places. The painting was excellent because it was so detailed.' (Girl, 8 years)

Work continued on the painting for the following three weeks. The younger children built up their own large pictures using chalks to develop the sky. They were encouraged to use their fingers to see how the chalks would blend and change shade. Castles were added using collage where shade and texture were explored and finally figures were added using pen to explore line and shape.

The older children used gouache to paint their own pictures. They used their original drawings to aid their work and were encouraged to use the same palette of colours as the artist. The work was not begun until we had gone through much preliminary drama work and writing to explore atmosphere.

Conversation pieces also developed. Beautiful little interactions between groups: one person doggedly instructing another on how to skate; gossiping neighbours and even a class statement about the castle rich and the labouring poor.

Our music student and music co-ordinator also worked on compositions to accompany the stories and the picture. These were taped and played back whilst stories were read over the top.

Where next? In the autumn we shall return to the picture and develop print making, hopefully covering monoprints, lino cuts and silk screen.'

Headmaster

'Small photocopied extracts of the painting were given to the children and they were challenged to make drawings to extend them in their own way.' Children 9–11 years

Following his 'extended extract' this boy chose to make a drawing of his own

113

Jan Beerstraten, 'The Castle at Muiden'

Paintings. Interpretations of the mood and feelings of the castle. Children 9–11 years

Paintings. Interpretations of the mood and feelings of the castle. Children 9–11 years

The younger children enjoyed the painting too, and built up their responses in four stages.

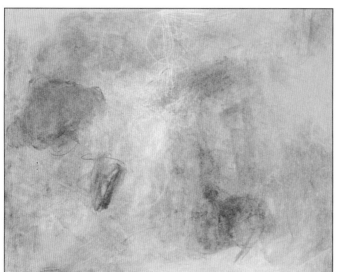

1 An all over general feel of the mood of the picture

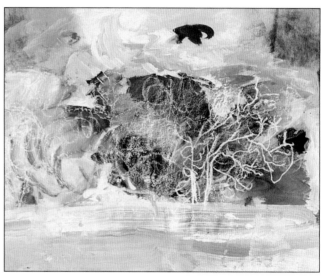

2 Heightening the mood by painting and drawing into it

3 and 4 Drawing and collaging a castle, then sticking it onto the picture and adding drawn and painted finishing touches

SHAPE AND GUSTAV KLIMT
9 year olds

'The Klimt project followed a preliminary project dealing with the elements of shape. Work included:

1 Taking a regular shape, exploding, repeating, distorting, rotating and overlapping it using black on white or white on black.

2 A shape hunt, looking for shapes in the environment. These were recorded in sketchbooks and discussed.

3 Designing a motif and using it in a variety of ways, exploring various media and techniques. Limits were set, for example three shapes and one line.

4 Once the children had achieved an interesting design they were encouraged to explore it using a range of media and techniques. The teacher's role was to offer advice, encouragement and technical support. Individual teaching was interspersed with short whole-class teaching sessions on techniques.

5 Children mounted and displayed a series of at least four variations of their motif.

Following this it was considered that Gustav Klimt was an appropriate artist to extend the experience of shape and introduce colour.

The activities included:

1 Introduction to the work of Klimt using reproductions and discussing shapes, colours, subject matter and the motifs.

2 The children divided an A4 sheet of paper into six sections and filled each section with a shape or motif taken from Klimt's painting.

3 A motif was selected from one of the paintings to look at the variety of ways in which Klimt developed it, and how they vary. The children were encouraged to produce a series of their own using various media and techniques.

4 Surface printing. This was a challenge to design a tablecloth or pillow case for Klimt.

5 Some of the children selected shapes and motifs from Klimt's work and transposed it into a three-dimensional card sculpture.

6 A 'window' or viewfinder was used to isolate a small section of the painting and reproduce it through drawing, painting or collage.

7 Finally the children were challenged to draw a clothed model using various shapes and motifs to describe clothing, background and furniture.'

Class teacher

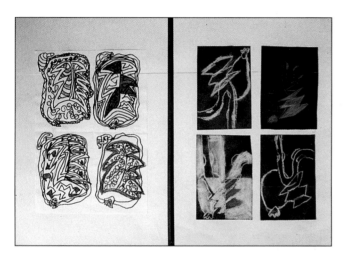

Work on shape by 9 year olds which preceded and informed a project on Gustav Klimt

KLIMT (continued)

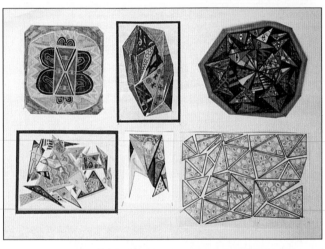

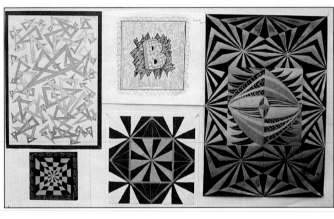

Work using a range of media, produced by 9 year olds following a project on shape and stimulated by a study of Gustav Klimt

CHARACTERS

Portraiture can be one of the most lively forms of art. At best it is based on sensitive insight and observation. Where character and characteristics are really considered, children can make strong statements, and can use the elements of art to good effect.

Boy, 12 years. 38 x 30

Girl, 5 years. 35 x 28 cms

Girl, 6 years. 35 x 24 cms

Girl, 13 years. 45 x 35 cms

Girl 13 years, 45 x 35 cms

Girl, 13 years. 35 x 24 cms

CHARACTERS

Reflection in tin foil. Boy,
13 years. 38 x 25 cms

Boy, 13 years. 35 x 32 cms

Girl, 13 years. 30 x 20 cms

Girl, 12 years. 15 cms high

Girl, 12 years. 15 x 12 cms

MOSAICS
12 years

Knowledge and Understanding

'The sheer scale, colour and amount of time represented by each small detailed area of tesserae make mosaics a seductive source material.

As with any theme the possibilities and range of examples are plentiful, crossing many centuries, styles and traditions. I decided to give the children insight into the transition of Roman mosaics, from the secular celebration of everyday life to the stylised, symbolic images created by the early Christian artists.

I believe that an important role of the art teacher is to provide the necessary knowledge for pupils to place art within a meaningful context. After discussing and analysing examples of both secular and religious mosaics pupils were able to give reasons why they thought there had been a shift in style from naturalism to stylised symbolic convention.

Through pinpointing visual codes and conventions in a contemporary garage forecourt setting, the class gained a better understanding of the different needs of the clients who lay behind the images they had seen. The emperor about to decorate his villa was concerned with grandeur and elegance, whereas the early Christian artist was duty bound to produce simple images. 'Painting can do for the illiterate what writing can do for those who can read,' said Pope Gregory the Great, and only strictly essential compositional elements were included.

Through analysing and gaining knowledge about the images in front of them, pupils were able to discuss, using specialist vocabulary, the reasons for this shift in style and emphasis. In a very tangible way we were able to discuss symbolism, metaphor, communication, naturalism, convention of scale and stylisation.

Investigating and Making

The challenge was to produce a mosaic with each of a class of twelve year old pupils. I experimented with a variety of approaches and decided that printing with carved ends of dowelling rods was a useful way of working. The design itself should involve a study of the method of mosaic making with carefully placed tesserae

The scheme of work fell into two stages – drawing, and printing with colour.

Drawing

Using each other as models the pupils made a carefully observed portrait drawing. They were encouraged throughout to look carefully at character, proportion and form.

Having studied large details of mosaics and Henry Moore's shelter drawings with their strong contour lines suggesting form, the pupils used tracing paper overlays placed on their drawings and developed them by building up contour lines suggesting relief.

The drawings were proportionally enlarged to A3 size and the colour of the paper base decided. We then discussed mark making and the need for selection in choosing the appropriate size and shaped stick for the painting task.

Printing and colour

Before the pupils started work, a demonstration and exploration of the effects of light on colour was undertaken producing simple variations of tone, and discussion of the ways in which shades and tones were affected took place.

The printing process developed these ideas further and the pupils assessed the visual effects of the work.'

Art teacher

MOSAICS

Portrait drawing from observation

Development into mosaic

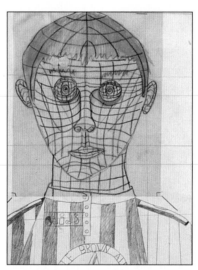

Contour lines. Tracing paper overlay

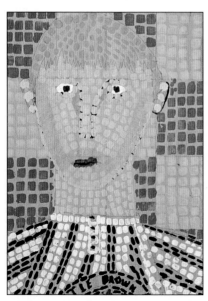

Printed mosaic

TRIPTYCHS (p 124)

Triptych study 1

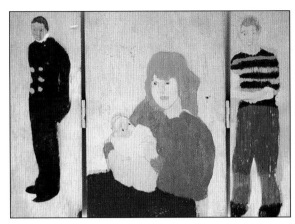

Hinged wooden triptych 1

Study of medieval triptych and gold leaf study for triptych 2

Preparatory studies for triptych 2

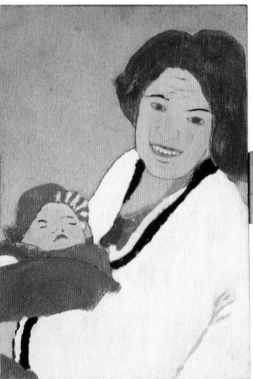

Hinged wooden triptych 2

TRIPTYCHS
13 years

'With this scheme of work I aimed to approach painting in what I consider to be an accessible way. Children enjoy making objects, so the late medieval/early renaissance vehicle of the triptych was ideal.

Knowledge and understanding

Using worksheets combining facts and questions, we discussed the history of triptychs and their compositional conventions and format.

Questions arose like: 'Why is the central figure bigger than the rest? Is it the most important?' Then we tried to work out why gold had been used and were able at this stage to discuss the idea of a visual metaphor to create, in this case, visions of a divine world.

We are used to thinking of works of art as the product of a sole author, so it was interesting for the pupils to learn about the guild/workshop structure in late medieval Italy.

We learnt how paints would be prepared by an apprentice from ground minerals and egg white. The surface to be painted would be carefully prepared with cloth, plaster, clay and gold leaf. By examining art from the past we were able to see in one small instance the effect technology has on art.

Investigating and making

For our triptych designs we used the theme of our family, and the pupils were asked to select suitable family photographs, using the format and conventions that they had seen. The most important image was to be the largest and take the central position, while the less valued images were to be placed smaller on the outside panels. The image and layout were worked out in sketchbooks.

I had managed to secure enough recycled wood to allow us all to make hinged triptychs which were substantial and offered the opportunity for us to paint on different material. We copied the images from the photographs on to the wood following the conventions.

Working on such a small scale stretched many pupils' paint and brush control but the careful preparation of the drawings and promise of gold paint led to great determination and mastering of trembling hands. As revision and development of previous painting experience I had also asked them to use a minimum of three tones per colour.

Finally we produced stencils to mask out the painted images and sprayed the wood gold for an authentic finish, using the idea of visual metaphor.

The triptychs were taken home and became the focus of much discussion.'

Class teacher

A CONTAINER AND ITS CONTENTS AS A SELF PORTRAIT
11 and 12 years

Objectives

To create a container/box and contents which reflect your own personality and character.

To consider how, through the manipulation of the elements of art, different emotions can be evoked or created.

To extend the pupils' understanding of expressive combinations of colour, texture, pattern, shape and form in a three-dimensional context.

To investigate concepts of abstract art.

Resources

Old cardboard boxes (good quality supermarket packaging), brown gummed tape, masking tape, variety of constructional materials, PVA, paint.

Examples of different types of containers and vessels.

Examples of abstract and expressionist works of art – for example Mark Rothko and Wassily Kandinsky.

Sketchbooks (zig zag form slotting into covers)

Casket and varied forms

Stage 1: Sketchbook work. Investigating and researching ideas and materials

- Pupils were asked to discuss and write about themselves – character, hobbies, home life.
- Self-portrait work. Pupils collected photographs of themselves when younger.
- Discussion and analysis of a selection of paintings where colour had been used in an expressive way, drawing attention to qualities and texture of paint, and surface characteristics.
- Samples of a range of colours were analysed by the pupils.
- Abstract collages were produced to reflect different aspects of personal character and mood.
- There were experiments with different textures in order to create character and mood in a tactile way. Pupils produced 'touch and feel' samples, selecting a wide variety of materials. Sheets were annotated with written responses of how the textures made them feel. (Examples of materials: sandpaper, coiled wire, polystyrene, wool, paper, card.)

Stage 2: Planning and researching in three dimensions

- The possible range of types of container was discussed. Consideration of how the shape and structure could reflect the individual pupil and the possibility of how significant objects could be placed inside the container was considered.
- Different facets of the box, exterior and interior could represent different moods, characteristics, memories or events.
- Maquettes and experimental constructions were made to help planning in three dimensions. Techniques such as cutting, scoring, ways of making hinges and templates were introduced.
- Design sheets were completed indicating ideas about form, colour, texture and the use of materials.

Stage 3: Making and constructing the final piece

Pupils made individual containers using the appropriate skills, and manipulating the formal, abstract, and expressive qualities for their particular purposes.

Stage 4

Evaluation – staff and pupil

- Sketchbooks and containers were discussed, evaluated and assessed.
- Pupils and staff were pleased overall with the outcomes.
- There was agreement that highly personal items had been created, and that the pupils felt a great sense of ownership.
- Staff felt that they had learned a great deal about individual pupils.
- Staff and pupils felt they had gained much through seeing and valuing differences in approach, selection and outcome, and that the project was a good vehicle to celebrate multi cultural diversity.'

Art teacher

A CONTAINER (continued)

Casket and supporting works

Varied forms

Varied forms

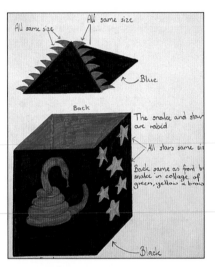

Design sheet

The finished box

Box and background studies

METAMORPHOSIS
13 years
Changing shapes

This project began with a self portrait considering character and characteristics. Following this drawing the pupils were asked to think of an animal or bird they felt they could identify with. This was extended by research into the particular creature through art forms and photographs.

The pupils were challenged to combine these drawings, having looked at the work of the visionary American painter Keith Powell. The background to their portrait was made up of chosen colours and apt words to describe their own characteristics.

Bibliography

Fulton J, *Materials in Design and Technology*, Design Council, 1992

Gentle K, *Children and Art Teaching*, Croom Helm, 1985

Gentle K, *Teaching Painting in the Primary School*, Cassell, 1993

Goodnow J, *Children's Drawings*, Fontana Open Books, 1997

HMSO Dept For Education, *Art in the National Curriculum, England*, 1995

HMSO Welsh Office Dept For Education, *Art in the National Curriculum, Wales*, 1995

Kellogg R, *Analysing Children's Art*, National Press Books (California), 1972

Manners N, *Three Dimensional Experience*, Hodder & Stoughton, 1995

Morgan M (Ed), *Art 4–11*, Stanley Thornes, 1987

Morgan M, *Art in Practice*, Nash Pollock Publishing, 1993

Paine S (Ed), *Six Children Draw*, Academic Press, 1981

Robertson S M, *Creative Crafts in Education*, Routledge & Kegan Paul, 1952

Roberston S M, *Rosegarden and Labyrinth*, Spring Publications (USA), 1991

Robinson G, *Sketchbooks: Explore and Store*, Hodder & Stoughton, 1995

Sedgewick D & F, *Drawing to Learn*, Hodder & Stoughton, 1993

Sedgewick D & F, *Art Across The Curriculum*, Hodder & Stoughton, 1996

Stevens K, *Learning Through Art and Artefacts*, Hodder & Stoughton, 1994

Taylor R, *Educating for Art*, Longman, 1986

The Scottish Office Education Dept, *Curriculum & Assessment in Scotland. National Guidelines – Expressive Arts 5–14*, 1992